Edward Johnston

Formal Penmanship

and other papers

edited by Heather Child

A PENTALIC BOOK
TAPLINGER PUBLISHING COMPANY
New York

Contents

Acknowledgements

I should like to thank all who have allowed their manuscripts by Edward Johnston to be illustrated in *Formal Penmanship* and the British Museum and the Victoria & Albert Museum for permission to reproduce from their collections. Also the Society of Designer-Craftsmen for permission to reprint *An Addendum to a Paper on the Labelling of Exhibits*; The Monotype Corporation for permission to quote from *Fifty Years On* and Sir Isaac Pitman & Co. for permission to quote from the Author's Preface to *Writing & Illuminating, & Lettering*. I should like to express my appreciation to Mr John Dreyfus for his interest and advice. In particular I should like to thank Margaret Alexander, Dorothy Mahoney, and Irene Wellington, one time students and friends of Edward Johnston, for reading the text and for their many helpful suggestions; also Ann Camp for her constructive help and Joan Pilsbury for her practical assistance.

H.C.

Foreword

Formal Penmanship was written by my father, Edward Johnston, during the last fifteen years of his life and was left unfinished when he died. For this reason I want to give what I can of his intentions and comments in regard to it, with a very brief account of his life and work. I should apologize to those who have read what I have written about him before[1] for some unavoidable repetition, but since memories are always shorter than authors like to imagine, this may not be necessary.

Johnston was of Scottish descent but for an English grandmother, a daughter of Sir Thomas Fowell Buxton, the 'liberator' of the slaves. Through her he was related to all the East Anglian Quaker families and inherited something of their traditions. He was bred to the idea of a life devoted to service and to a search for truth. To him religion, life and work were inseparable.

He was born in Uruguay in 1872, where his ne'er-do-well father was ranching at the time. They soon returned to England but they never again had a settled home, nor did the children ever go to school. They were keen readers, however, and largely educated themselves. Later Edward studied medicine at Edinburgh but gave this up in 1898, at the age of 26, to study art.

He arrived in London when the Arts and Crafts revival was at its height and immediately came under the influence of W. R. Lethaby, founder and Principal of the Central School of Arts and Crafts. It was Lethaby who suggested that he should take up calligraphy, after seeing some manuscripts that he had attempted. It was an instance of the intuition for which Lethaby was noted that at only their second meeting he disconcerted Johnston by telling him that he, who had come to learn, was, instead, to *teach* calligraphy at the Central School, where as yet there was no such class. Meanwhile he was advised to study early manuscripts at the British Museum. 'Luckily for me', he said, 'there was no one to teach me because no one knew anything about my subject.' In fact calligraphy was truly a lost art, having disappeared with the invention of printing. It had not even a name. Such work as was being done at the time was referred to and thought of as 'illumination' and was foredoomed to lifelessness, being an attempt to copy appearances without understanding techniques. Johnston, by his study of early manuscripts, rediscovered the techniques for himself. His ambition was 'to make *living letters* with a formal pen'. Years later he said 'Our aim should be, I think, to make letters live . . . that men themselves may have more life'.

Johnston began teaching at the Central School in 1899. He proved an inspiring teacher and was much loved by his students, never more so than by the seven in his first class, among whom were Noel Rooke and Eric Gill. Soon he had a second class at Camberwell and then another at the Royal College of Art, where he taught for the next thirty years.

[1] *Edward Johnston*, Priscilla Johnston, Faber & Faber, 1959.

His book, *Writing & Illuminating, & Lettering*, begun about this time, took him nearly four years of most strenuous and concentrated work. It was published in 1906 in the *Artistic Crafts Series* edited by Lethaby and remains to this day the leading text-book on the subject. To begin with he wrote and taught a hand he described as a 'modernized half-uncial' but after a few years this was superseded by his 'foundational hand', based on tenth-century models, in which most of his work was done for the greater part of his life. Then, quite suddenly, after nearly twenty years, he evolved an entirely new form, bold and compressed, influenced by sixteenth-century Italic.

In 1903 he had married, a marriage which was his unfailing support for more than thirty years. His wife let him go his own intractable way and never tried to make him tidy, punctual, or businesslike, as his relatives had so ardently hoped that she might and his friends so much feared that she would. He had his own unusual ways of doing almost everything and was a most inconvenient man to be married to, but, like his students, only with more to contend with, she continued to be devoted to him.

The schedule of his life's achievements which Johnston composed for *Who's Who* in 1937 listed three main items in his career: '*Studied penshapes of letters in early manuscripts, British Museum*' – 'Teacher of *the first classes* in formal penmanship and lettering' and 'Designed block letter *based on classical Roman capital* proportions'. 'I claim no particular merit in myself', he said of these entries, 'but – historically – it happens that I have been the pioneer in three rather simple and, indeed rather obvious, ideas, which – technically – have become of some importance.' The block letter was designed for the Underground Railways and was a private type for their use only. When, a few years later, Eric Gill designed what was virtually the same alphabet, 'owing', as he told Johnston, 'all its goodness to your Underground letter', and it became generally available under the name of *Gill Sans*, its success was meteoric and its influence worldwide.

In 1929 Johnston was persuaded to spend part of the winter abroad with his wife for the sake of their health. He disliked being away from home and from his own things, but he bought a cheap writing-block in San Remo and began, at last, to write a book that had been in his mind for many years. His first book on calligraphy had been published twenty-three years before, at the start of his working life, and now, when nearing the end of it, he decided to try to set down something of all that he had learnt since. It was to be in two parts, Part I dealing with the practical aspects of Formal Penmanship and Part II with the theoretical side, and, one had hoped, perhaps disclosing something of his philosophy. In particular he had felt the need to 'try to *face fundamental things*', he said, and to help others to do so. The book progressed so slowly however, that, though he worked on it for fifteen years, Part II was never reached. The beginning was a matter of extreme difficulty and the first chapter, worked over for ten years, grew ever longer and developed so many interpolations that in the end he decided to make it Part I and let subsequent chapters form further parts. The original two parts planned might thus, in the end, have come to be regarded as two Books.

In February 1937 he wrote to me: 'On the 6th January, while indexing 2nd section of the Notebook, I lit on *the most hopeful plan* yet for opening chapter I (the problem which has wrestled with me for over three years). And I look forward to trying to carry *this* out fairly soon.'

More than three and a half years later, in November 1940, he wrote to his daughter Barbara: 'Perhaps you know, perhaps not, how long I have puzzled over the question *at what point* in my Book and *how much* (*and how expressed*) should I reveal vital factors in Formal Penmanship. It is a kind of Paradox of Teaching or Learning – To know how to make Things you must make them – ("practising" teaches you how to practise – or, rather, how to do practising) but the student cannot make things (we say) until he has learnt how to make them. The solution (of How, then, does he learn?) is found in the theorem (or argument by the Schoolmen, I think) Achilles cannot cross a Room, for before he crosses R he must cross $\frac{R}{2}$ and before he crosses the remaining $\frac{R}{2}$ he must cross $\frac{\frac{R}{2}}{2}$ and so on, leaving a fraction always to be crossed. The answer may be found in the fact that Achilles does actually cross it, or, in the Act *itself*, which goes by strides or *jumps* (not stopping to recognise the perpetual decimal left).

'Then the teacher must give vital information in that form, namely partly apprehensible and remainderly jumpable. Now, since 1933 I have stuck over this question and see-sawed over it. In 1934 I decided there must be an "early reference to the three Writing Conditions" and stopped drafting further to write an interpolation. This was to be just a note, but I spent two months that summer over it and produced 17 pp. of typewriting and figs. Naturally I had a reaction (feeling that the s. wd. die of indigestion) and postponed it. And so, year after year since then (and you know what some of the years have been)[1] I have doubted and felt held up. (In '37 and '38 I wrote a 14 p. section for insertion later in the chapter, taking several months). But, having put that section away in my pocket – like your letter and several other letters – I tried to get the *beginning* made, without any reference to it. In the summer of this year I tried short notes and again abandoned them but *somehow got in a good and fairly short par*. . . . Then about the end of this Aug. or beginning of October, again I felt it *must* be done, and it began to work out happily (attached to the good, short par.). When your letter came . . . I was at a kind of constructive crisis and felt it must be gone through with, even breaking my life's rule about acknowledging money. Since then there has been a slow but pretty sure advance (indicated to some extent by the fact that this very morning I decided that the original *chapter I* of about 10 years ago, which split up into three distinct chapters about 7 or 8 years ago, should split into 6 reasonable length chapters and together form *Part One*. Old chaps. II and III will probably follow and become PARTS.'

The letter ends with a diagram of 'typical stroke shapes produced by simple movements of the formal pen' as shown in his book. These strokes are more or less vertical and close together with the white background making clear-cut shapes between them. Under the figure he has scribbled 'This is symbolic of a sort of vision which I had the other day – I think I see the light between the trees at last'.

Another reference to the book in a letter helps to explain why the rate of progress was slow: 'You will understand why this is short when I say that I have this moment composed the following sentence. "He cuts the NIB of the pen to a special shape." – and let us hope it is permanently composed because planning to use that remark appears to have taken twelve weeks.'

[1] The work was frequently held up by ill-health.

When asked, once, how he had ever managed to finish his first book, Johnston answered 'It was comparatively easy then because I knew nothing about the subject.' Recalling those days he spoke of 'the almost irrecoverable serenity of inexperience', contrasted with the 'not-without-comfort-and-joy travail of my present Book'. The first book had been 'a congenial Task', he said, but the second was 'not a Task but a Quest . . . an absorbing Quest'. The object of the first was 'to hand over a little simple knowledge', of the second 'to tell, if it be possible, some beliefs and hopes'.

At his rate of progress this was, alas, not possible, but what he was able to set down on paper is now at last being published. It was originally edited by Violet Hawkes, who had been Johnston's assistant at the Royal College of Art, but for various reasons this version was eventually withdrawn, after much devoted work had been put into it. *Formal Penmanship* has now been edited entirely anew by Heather Child, herself a calligrapher of repute, whose wide experience of literary work combined with her scrupulous accuracy have made her, in our view, a most happy choice.

Priscilla Johnston

Editor's Introduction

That modern calligraphy ever rose like a phoenix from the ashes of forgotten crafts was largely due to Edward Johnston. It is to his perception of fundamentals that formal penmanship owes its life and continuing tradition today.

In his own words 'Developing, or rather *re*-developing, an art involves *the tracing in one's own experience of a process resembling its past development*. And it is by such a course that we, who wish to revive Writing and Illuminating, may renew them, evolving new methods and traditions for ourselves, till at length we attain a modern and beautiful technique. And if we would be more than amateurs, we must study and practise *the making of beautiful THINGS* and thereby gain experience of Tools, Materials and Methods.'[1]

In October 1898 Sydney Cockerell, later Sir Sydney, a notable authority on illuminated manuscripts, and at one time secretary and close friend of William Morris, showed Johnston early manuscripts in the British Museum, stressing particularly the exemplary qualities of Winchester scripts of the tenth and eleventh centuries which he considered 'most worthy of the attention of a potential scribe'. No one could have foreseen how far-reaching Johnston's ensuing studies would be, or what a wealth of craftsmanship would stem from his profound analysis of these scripts; for at that time the tradition of good lettering was at its nadir. It was his apparently simple discovery that 'the nature and form of a letter is determined by the nature and form of the tool that makes it, and that the breadth of the letter-stroke is in direct ratio to the breadth of the nib's edge' which laid the whole foundation of modern calligraphy. People supposed that medieval letter forms were drawn in outline and the strokes filled in. It was not understood that the shape of the tool and the action of the hand holding it made each letter-stroke in one gesture.

Edward Johnston's early teaching is well known to students of calligraphy from his classic and instructive manual *Writing & Illuminating, & Lettering*, first published in 1906, now in its thirtieth impression and still essential reading for craftsmen of lettering today.

Johnston began to write *Formal Penmanship* in 1929 and well before that it had been his intention to write a book to show the development of his ideas and reflections, stemming from his years of teaching and practical experience. In 1937 he wrote 'The primary object of the book is to make an explicit statement on the art of Formal Penmanship and after thirty years of experience and practice to give a more assured view than in my first book *Writing & Illuminating, & Lettering*.'[2] He felt that although scribes were working with skill and facility they were sometimes unaware of essentials. When he died in 1944, however, his book was still incomplete.

The material for *Formal Penmanship* has not been published before and it

---

[1] *Writing & Illuminating, & Lettering.*
[2] Quoted from Edward Johnston's vellum-bound notebook.

has been the present editor's task to put in order and prepare for publication Edward Johnston's papers and diagrams, so that although unfinished, they may appear in book form, for the benefit of those interested in the fundamental development of formal writing and particularly those concerned with perpetuating its practice.

.It has been a happy suggestion to include seven of the articles Johnston wrote in 1913 for the shortlived journal *The Imprint*, a periodical whose influence was out of all proportion to its life span. These have been placed before the text of *Formal Penmanship* as they were written earlier.

The *Addendum to a Paper on the Labelling of Exhibits*, 1933, in which he describes his calligraphic manuscript of Shakespeare's Sonnet CXVI, is also reprinted in the present volume, and this fine sonnet is illustrated in colour as the Frontispiece.

The full meaning of the illustrations will only be comprehended by closely following the text. They range from the explanatory figures in the text of *The Imprint* and *Formal Penmanship*, to the wide variety of Johnston's own manuscript work reproduced in the twenty-three plates. The juxtaposition of illustrations demonstrating his teaching methods together with those of his own calligraphy is a valuable record of his thought and achievement as a teacher and a craftsman.

The text of Formal Penmanship

The original material for the treatise of *Formal Penmanship* consists of 163 quarto pages of handwriting and typescript; many of the pages contain copious notes, interpolations and amendments to the text, and only some of these are dated. There are more than fifty-three diagrams in the text made by Johnston in pencil and ordinary blue ink.

Prolonged and searching consideration was given to everything Johnston wrote; he worked and reworked each sentence, striving for maximum clarity. This struggle to express his thoughts with intensity and lucidity caused him to make multiple versions of the main ideas in his mind, and to plan and replan the construction of the book as time went on. Parts of the book are fragmentary, almost all of it is incomplete, but much of the thought is concentrated in a few trenchant phrases. It is clear that by 1942 he had intended to divide the book into parts, with chapters and sub-sections, but in fact only Chapters 1 and 2 were numbered.

In Part I, 'Formal Penmanship described by its TOOLS', Johnston is concerned with what he terms the weight-angle-form complex and he develops his theme that the three primary factors, or writing conditions, are the weight of the stroke, the angle of the pen, and the form of the letter. In Part II, 'Formal Penmanship defined by its TRADITIONS', he discusses the importance to the modern scribe of the study of specific hands in early manuscripts. In Part III, 'Formal Penmanship described by the THING', Johnston sets out the underlying principles and beliefs he sees to be implicit in the approach of the scribe to his work, whether it is the scribe of the past or the scribe of today. These explicit statements are a testimony for his whole life's work, and for that reason I should, as editor, like to draw particular attention to this part. Since it explains so much of the purpose of the book some readers may prefer to begin with it, before reading his more analytical thoughts on the construction and development of letters. Part III would then be virtually an introduction to Johnston's approach to his subject, which *The Imprint* articles and Parts I and II of *Formal Penmanship* develop and explain in detail.

In editing this material my purpose has been to produce a consecutive text representing the latest draft of *Formal Penmanship*. It is important that the original text should be published as Johnston wrote it and nowhere have I altered his wording, except to choose between alternative versions of a statement and to cut out marginal notes where these are no longer relevant.

I have studied two of Johnston's notebooks, one inscribed 'Edward Johnston Cleves, Ditchling, Sx. (valuable notes from August 1920)'; the other a remarkable notebook bound by him in classic vellum which contains four sections each with an index and about a hundred pages ($7 \times 3\frac{1}{2}$ in.) closely packed with meticulously dated (1936–9) wide-ranging notes, quotations and jottings. Studying these notes has been most rewarding for they reveal more clearly than any other material the quality of Johnston's mind. Many of the entries relate to penmanship and to his proposed book and its construction. These have been taken into account in editing this work, for one of the more difficult problems has been to choose the best arrangement of chapters and sub-sections; a problem that appears to have been almost insuperable to Johnston himself. Discussing his work with Irene Wellington, his former student and friend of many years, has been invaluable to me. Her knowledge of the subject and first-hand experience of Johnston's aims and methods have enabled her to clarify some of the more obscure points in his manuscript.

In the original text there are several variant drafts of sections in Part I. I have put these versions together and included almost all the diagrams, even where some of these are similar to one another. Certain overlapping is unavoidable and the fragmentary nature of many of the sections tends to make a rather disjointed whole. It was a feature of Johnston's writing that he repeated a point he wished to make in order to give it emphasis. The remark of the priest, recorded by Johnston in his 'vellum-bound notebook', makes the point: 'First I tell them what I am going to tell them. Then I tell them. Then I tell them what I have told them.'

Johnston himself said 'There is nothing so unemphatic as over-emphasis'; nevertheless he had original theories on the layout of the text. His passion for clarity in his writing was sometimes obscured by emphasis expressed by his use of capitals, inverted commas, underlinings and the like. In my transcription I have discarded certain of these forms, particularly the capital letters; although vivid when handwritten, on the printed page they produce a sense of strain which is distracting to the reader.

The text figures in Formal Penmanship

In 1937 Johnston wrote 'General idea for the book, many figures and few but pithy words' and 'As far as possible each sub-section to have at least one figure'.[1]

In the original manuscript these clear, bold diagrams, associated on some pages with his firm handwriting, have vitality and charm; however, whether they are written in blue ink or with the delicacy of double-pencils, they must be taken at this stage as indications of his thought – reminders to himself of what he wanted to illustrate in each figure and explain in its caption rather than final statements. For instance, he states categorically that the pen angle is 30° or 45°, and writes 'We must keep the slant of the pen uniform', but there is often a discrepancy between the statement which is sound and the relevant diagram. This discrepancy may be partly accounted for by the fact that, as he grew more frail, he sometimes worked in bed with a board on his knees and the unusually large scale of some diagrams could be the result of changing eyesight.

Here the tension lies in the difference between an exemplar and the free interpretation of it; spontaneous writing is dependent on the free movement of the hand and on the subject of exemplars Johnston wrote: 'But if an alphabet be written as a SPECIMEN it is primarily a specimen Alphabet (and is debarred from that natural freedom or run of free writing – *Brushed by the feathers of an Angel's wing in passing* – debarred from those varieties, differences, faults – which are not real faults in free writing) it becomes by comparison Artificial.'[1]

The correct pen angle is of prime importance in teaching and if the diagrams had been reproduced from the originals some of them might have led to confusion. This point has been brought home to me in discussion of the text and the figures with Ann Camp, a scribe whose study of first principles and wide knowledge of the craft makes her an outstanding teacher of lettering and calligraphy. The fifty-three figures in *Formal Penmanship* have therefore been redrawn in a form suitable for line-block reproduction by Joan Pilsbury, herself a distinguished scribe working in the Johnston tradition. Her aim has been to make as exact a statement as possible of his logical intention, checking the pen angles in the diagrams with the wording of the text. This has seemed a legitimate course to take since the diagrams were never completed in a form intended for publication, and the method of reproduction had not been considered at that stage by Johnston himself.

Representative pages from the original manuscript and several of the figures are reproduced facsimile on plates 1–4. These reproductions render something of the spirit and authority of Johnston's writing and vigour of his diagrams. They also illustrate a few of the editor's problems in unravelling the text.

Edward Johnston's notes for his Preface

Formal Penmanship was not far enough advanced at the time of Johnston's death for him to have written his Author's Preface, but there are elucidating entries in his vellum-bound notebook for 1937 and 1938, recording some of the points he intended to make, here quoted:

'The important things for the Preface are: (1) The reasons for the book. (2) Its scope. The difference with "W.&I.&L." come under 1. (3) The idea of application of F.P. and careful study of creative forms (Roman ABC); the modern intelligent craftsman, his chances of occupational and educational gain at least. (4) To save the craft from oblivion.'

'This (F.P.) was projected as a lesson or teaching book and does its best to give a tangible doctrine of a special craft. "W.&I.&L." contained more generalities and I projected it rather as a reference book for Penmen and Letterers.'

'Note for the opening para. of Preface: There are three questions that every

[1]Vellum-bound notebook.

honest and truly practical man must ask of Things. *What* is the Thing? *How* is it done? *Why* should it be done?'

'Reasons for writing this book (in these days when less interest in Arts and Crafts and more in mechanics), while we continue to read by means of the letters of the Alphabet, letter-design and treatment will continue important and (current and recurring) F.P. is the source of these and remains the best authority and guide. F.P. is one of the simplest crafts to grasp, at least its historical development, its present use and practice and its possibilities. It is a simple clue to fundamentals of other crafts and the theory of Design, and for those who like it, it offers not too difficult work of absorbing interest.'

'After all the problem before us is fairly simple: *To make good letters and arrange them well.*'

'Note for the Preface: If I may criticise the majority of modern Formal Penmen's MS work (students, many of them my own students that I must have failed to teach) it is that their penmanship is lacking fundamental techniques. The Three Primary Conditions do not seem to be grasped, or observed, or understood. Weight, Angle and Letter Form all seem to be chanced rather than chosen, and all at the mercy of a rather imperfect writing surface. Perhaps the failure is deeper and more general and is really a failure to appreciate the Three Essential Qualities of Sharpness, Unity and Freedom. Here, I think, is the clue to putting the matter right – cultivate Sharpness; and the Form, Angle and Weight all become Explicit. A form that is sharp and clean-cut may be faulty but not slovenly or vague. And to cultivate Unity and Freedom will bring one into a right tradition, lift one out of the rut of indifference and the blind alley of copying and will enable one to imitate the goodness and heart of Things and bring one into a good Tradition.'

The scribe of today is often misled by trying to copy Johnston's personal scripts and copyists rarely produce spirited or vital work; for in order to write well one must work from a genuine understanding of letter forms as produced by the movements of the pen. Readers familiar with *Writing & Illuminating, & Lettering* will recall that Johnston in his author's Preface wrote:

'As "copy book" hands, simple, primitive, pen-forms – such as the Uncial or Half-Uncial – afford the best training and permit the cultivation of the freedom which is essential in writing; they prepare the way for the mastery of the most practical characters – the ROMAN CAPITAL, roman small letter, and italic – and the ultimate development of a lively and personal penmanship.'

The meaning of Formal Penmanship

In the writing of *Formal Penmanship* Johnston set out on an unending quest – the image and meaning of penmanship which he had in his mind was based on a profound understanding of historic hands which he absorbed through patient study, mathematical analysis and a craftsman's intuitive insight. He admitted that the first stages of learning are imitative, but he never slavishly copied an early script. He grasped the underlying forms and principles, pondered them deeply and then wrote with unhesitating spontaneity. His own words evoke an ideal freedom: 'Within the limits of our craft we cannot have too much freedom; for too much fitting and planning makes the work lifeless, and it is conceivable that in the finest work the Rules are concealed, and that, for example, a MS might be most beautiful without ruled lines and methodical arrangement. But the more clearly we realise our limitations the more practical our work. And it is rather as a stimulus to definite thought – not as an embodiment of hard and fast rules – that various methodical plans and tables of analysis are given in this book. It is well to recognize at once, the fact that mere taking to pieces, or analysing, followed by "putting together", is only a means of becoming acquainted with the mechanism of construction, and will not reproduce the original beauty of a thing: it is an education for work, but all work which is honest and straight-forward has a beauty and freshness of its own.'[1]

Johnston chose a few very fine manuscripts as the basis of his study; he might well have chosen others, as one could today. He mastered those selected hands so thoroughly that he acquired from them the knowledge and skill to move on to greater freedom, producing highly personal styles. That was his genius. His exemplars and analyses in *Formal Penmanship* provide the key to understanding manuscript hands, but copying them will not on its own produce a work of art. Bare analysis can become pointless and void without creative synthesis of the whole task in hand. His aims were always objective and primarily controlled by the requirements of the Thing itself, its meaning and its purpose; again in his own words 'Following our craft rather than making it follow us'.[2]

To Johnston the most important consideration of a manuscript was the words and he saw clearly that the chief duty of the scribe was to express the author's meaning. However, he did not impose preconceived ideas on a manuscript and except about the sheer mathematical inevitability of pen strokes he was not inflexible. He could be flexible even about the factor of distinct legibility; this can be seen in the deliberate choice of black-letter to halt a too facile reading of his script of Shakespeare's sonnet CXVI. He believed that when a scribe has sufficiently matured to be himself his calligraphy will emerge in a personal and intuitive way. His own work is a witness to his belief that from their living roots in the past spring both the present and the future of the crafts 'For all things – materials, tools, methods – are waiting to serve us and we have only to find the "spell" that will set the whole universe a-making for us'.[3]

The Plates

The material for the plates has been chosen primarily to expand Johnston's statement that *Formal Penmanship* was projected as a lesson or teaching book. Secondly to show what can be learnt from the range and development of his personal styles of writing and craftsmanship.

Reproduction cannot convey the subtleties of craftsmanship or the tactile quality of materials and every effort should be made to see Johnston's original manuscripts, in order to realize just what he meant by sharpness of the pen on properly prepared vellum, and the nature of ink and colour powerfully contrasting and complementing each other.

Large classes of students posed a teaching problem for Johnston and he soon had to devise means of mass instruction. He illustrated his lectures at the Royal College of Art by demonstrating on the blackboard with broad chalk cut to a chisel edge; fortunately the blackboard was photographed by his assistant, Miss

[1] *Writing & Illuminating, & Lettering.*
[2] *Ibid.*
[3] *Ibid.*

Violet Hawkes, at the end of each session and it is regretted that this notable record of his teaching cannot be reproduced in *Formal Penmanship*. A set of photographic prints of these remarkable blackboard demonstrations may be consulted in the Victoria & Albert Museum Library and some of Johnston's manuscripts can also be seen there including *A Book of Sample Scripts*.

Plate 5 illustrates one of the Winchester Formal Writing Sheets; these were partly printed and partly handwritten by Johnston himself for the use of his students. Additional aids to his teaching were alphabet study-sheets duplicated by a hectograph method and versions exist in a variety of hands. These class-sheets were superseded by his portfolio *Manuscript & Inscription Letters* published by John Hogg in 1909.

The theory and practice of Johnston's teaching are nowhere more fascinatingly revealed than in the notebook he made for Margaret Alexander when she was a student taking private lessons, pages of which she has kindly allowed to be reproduced here.

Plates 6 and 7 are pages from Dorothy Mahoney's notebook and illustrate typical demonstrations made by Johnston with double-pencils for students attending his lettering class at the Royal College of Art. When his health began to fail Dorothy Mahoney carried on his class at the College. I am grateful to her for allowing these pages to be reproduced and for elucidating points in Johnston's teaching.

The plates concerned with Johnston's own calligraphy show something of the diversity of his formal hands. When *Writing & Illuminating, & Lettering* was first published he was writing and teaching a script he called a modernized half-uncial. This he considered a beautiful and a most exacting hand and therefore valuable as training. Before long, however, he developed his foundational hand, since he realized this was more appropriate and practical in relation to standards of legibility today. He therefore adopted it as the basis of his teaching and it was the hand in which he carried out the greater part of his manuscript work. His compressed form of the foundational hand, which has many pen lifts and which he termed a formal or heavy italic writing, was also developed from tenth-century book hands.

All through his work the interplay between his teaching and his set commissions is apparent. He stressed in his teaching that weight in letter-form, even over-weight, almost forces the student to observe the results of pen strokes and to realize the pattern-making qualities in both strokes and background, also that it is less easy to detect and analyse faults in writing of lighter weight. This factor of weight may have influenced his own work; as we see, his later writing becomes more decisive and vigorous. There may have been additional reasons for this but certainly the fascination of the edged-pen with its manifold possibilities led him continuously to experiment. For instance in the year 1924 Johnston was asked to complete the writing of a medieval manuscript, Gower's *Confessio Amantis*, of which the last page was missing, and this led him to research into fourteenth- and fifteenth-century English Book hands. Subsequently he chose these strong black-letter forms, when he was commissioned to write a page from Chaucer and later one from Barbour's *The Bruce*, and decided to use a hand contemporary with the text – 'In some such style as the following men first read Chaucer' he wrote on the MS. He used the strong Gothic capitals of this Chaucerian script in his Perpetual Calendar which is illustrated on plate 21, and again, in the text figures in Chapter 5 of *Formal Penmanship*.

At this time Johnston was also evolving an entirely new hand, a bold compressed style of writing with pointed arches to the letters and tenuous terminals to the ascending and descending strokes. This vital and original hand has been variously called a pointed 'italic', a sharpened 'italic' and a Gothicized 'italic'. Johnston wrote of the Keighley Roll of Honour, the first of his manuscripts in this compressed style and completed in 1924, 'The writing may be described as an "Italic hand", which I have evolved directly from a "book hand" in a Winchester MS of the 10th century (now in the British Museum) & modified in sympathy with 16th century Italic – evolved, that is to say, by using the pen in a natural manner, tending to produce the characteristics of italic writing, namely compression & branching.'[1]

It is interesting to consider Noel Rooke's observations on this style, quoted in Priscilla Johnston's book: 'It is not in any sense an italic . . . the origins are deeper and more structural.' He had discussed it with Johnston and he says: 'He saw that more compressed forms, getting more letters into the same length of line, could be an economy not only of space but of legibility. The distinction between a straight stroke and a curve is always a vital one. So he evolved a compressed hand which preserved the curves and avoided the width and slowness of the round-hands, yet was as economic of space and therefore of "eye-travel" as the Gothic hand. It seems most probable that, appreciating the reasons for compression, he set about obtaining the advantages without the disadvantages. That was, as I remember it, his line of discussion at the time.'[2]

The term Italic today has become more specifically associated with the Humanistic scripts of the Renaissance, and Johnston maintained that he had not fully researched into these; however, he taught that the true characteristics of italic are: lateral compression with a tendency to lengthened ascenders and descenders; branching of the arches of the letters; the slope associated with italic, but not essential to it, comes from speed of writing, see plate 8.

Towards the end of his life Johnston wrote a number of calligraphic letters to friends in a semi-formal hand, an outstanding feature of which was the bold initials of the recipient and sometimes the monogram E.J. One of the last of these is an eight-page letter to Paul Standard written in April 1944, six months before he died. Plates 12 and 13 show pages 3 and 4 which are most relevant to this book.

Processes of reproduction tend to blunt the sharpness of original writing, and the fine balance of red and black, which is a strong characteristic of many of Johnston's manuscripts, is unfortunately lost. Nevertheless in spite of these limitations the essential qualities of sharpness, unity and freedom are evident in the clean-cut, explicit form of the letters and in the uniform flow of the writing. His qualities as a craftsman are revealed in his sense of line, the breadth of his outlook and in his ability to criticize his own work. He took every possible care and thought in the preparation of a manuscript, but once the writing was set in motion it was the subject and the presentation of it that were of the greatest importance. In his own words: 'Only an attempt to do practical work will raise practical problems, and therefore *useful practice is the making of real and definite Things.*'[3]

Formal Penmanship is clearly only a fragment of the book Edward Johnston intended, but it contains in essence the fundamental principles of his later teaching. Its substance could be said to have emerged gradually in the fullness of time, the wide range of his thought maturing the content over the years, and it is this which gives the book such complete authority.

[1] Quoted from Edward Johnston's papers.
[2] *Edward Johnston*, Priscilla Johnston, Faber & Faber, 1959.
[3] *Writing & Illuminating, & Lettering.*

List of books

Writing & Illuminating, & Lettering
by Edward Johnston.
With diagrams and illustrations by the Author and Noel Rooke; an Appendix
on gilding by Graily Hewitt and an Appendix on Inscriptions in stone by
A. E. R. Gill.
In the Artistic Crafts Series of Technical Handbooks edited by W. R. Lethaby.
Sir Isaac Pitman & Sons Ltd.
First published by John Hogg, London, 1906.

Manuscript & Inscription Letters
by Edward Johnston.
With 5 plates by A. E. R. Gill.
A portfolio for schools and classes and for the use of craftsmen.
Published by John Hogg, London, 1909.

Tributes to Edward Johnston
Privately printed by permission of the Society of Scribes & Illuminators
at the Maidstone College of Art, 1948.

Edward Johnston
by Priscilla Johnston.
Published by Faber & Faber, 1959.

A Book of Sample Scripts
Reproduced in facsimile from Edward Johnston's manuscript made for
Sir Sydney Cockerell, under the title *The House of David, his Inheritance: a
Book of Sample Scripts*. The manuscript was completed in 1914 and is now in
the Victoria & Albert Museum Library, L.4391–1959.
Published by Her Majesty's Stationery Office for the Museum 1966.

The Imprint articles

Editor's Note: The Imprint articles

'In 1913 the entire story of *The Imprint* was staged in nine thrilling issues: scarcely a successful publishing venture if looked at from the point of view of longevity. Yet the influence exerted on typographical design by this brave vision has still to be evaluated.'

This clarion sentence from Monotype's *Fifty Years On*[1] is a tribute to the importance of the shortlived journal. It was essentially a printing journal, concerned with every aspect of the making of books and trade printing; its scholarly interests included calligraphy and methods of illumination. In the words of the founders its aim was 'to benefit and, if possible, elevate the printing and allied trades and to show the place for craftsmanship in the printing trade'.

The Imprint had four joint editors, all recognized authorities in their own field. Gerard T. Meynell was a director of the Westminster Press, which undertook the production of the journal. He was a first cousin of Francis Meynell of the Nonesuch Press, and a member of that distinguished literary family. His three co-editors were all lecturers at the LCC Central School of Arts and Crafts. J. H. Mason, who had been with the Doves Press, brought an encyclopaedic knowledge of printing techniques to his work in the publication. The influence of Edward Johnston is clearly evident. F. Ernest Jackson, the well-known lithographer and, later, principal of Byam Shaw School of Art, completed the editorial team. Supporting them was an advisory committee of thirty-two members, among them Professor W. R. Lethaby, Douglas Cockerell, C. H. St. John Hornby, Robert Bridges, Theodore L. de Vinne, R. A. Austen-Leigh and H. G. Webb, men of note in their own fields and in the graphic arts.

Imprint Old Face type, based on Caslon Old Face, was designed by J. H. Mason especially for the journal and produced by Lanston Monotype Corporation in a remarkably short time. Its distinction added to the visual quality of the journal and won good opinions from type designers, encouraging other adaptations of classical typefaces.

The title and border on the cover of *The Imprint* were written and drawn by Edward Johnston with the edged-pen and printed from line-blocks. His characteristic misgivings on the quality of the cover led him to publish a sort of apologia in the first number.

Johnston's chief contribution was a series of seven articles on the study and practice of penmanship, under the title 'Decoration and its uses', which are reprinted here in full. This series of articles shows the development of his thought and teaching since the publication of *Writing & Illuminating, & Lettering* seven years before, and it is interesting to note the first mention in print of his Foundational Hand. In the February number, which was devoted to children's books, he included drawings by his daughters aged 7 and 8 and a report of

[1] Published by The Monotype Corporation, 1963.

their views on book illustration. These are not reprinted in *Formal Penmanship*.

Johnston annotated one copy of *The Imprint* articles after publication, and I have reproduced his few manuscript additions in square brackets.

The first issue of *The Imprint* appeared in January 1913 and an edition of 10,000 copies was circulated. The technical and aesthetic standards were set high, by the taste, enthusiasm, and idealism of the editors. Subsequent numbers sustained the quality but the number of advertisers declined. January to June constituted the first volume; the second volume opened with the July number and continued with the handsome August issue, in which the then unknown Stanley A. Morison appeared as the author of an article on liturgical books. Publication then faltered, no numbers appeared in September or October; in November the last issue of *The Imprint* was published and no explanations for the collapse of the journal were put forward.

Decoration and its uses

These papers will deal chiefly with the decoration that is appropriate to books and letters, and, in particular, will consider what the modern craftsman may expect to get out of the study or practice of penmanship. But as the principles of decoration, which I hope to discover here, are in all crafts fundamentally alike, the larger title may be justified.

As the word decoration has become somewhat artificialized, not to say degraded, it is worth recalling its more primitive and exact meaning. I take the following definition of the verb from an ordinary standard dictionary (Annandale's Concise Dictionary, 1899):

Decorate, (L. *decoro, decoratum,* from *decus, decor,* comeliness, grace; akin *decent.*) To deck with something becoming or ornamental; to adorn; to beautify; to embellish. . . .

I should like to lay particular stress on the Latin derivation – comeliness and grace – and the kinship with the word decent.

Again, as the word use is one for which we all have a private interpretation and is therefore apt to be narrowed and ab-used, it is worth refreshing our memories with the wider sense of a dictionary definition. From the same dictionary I take the following:

Use, *n.* [O. Fr. *us,* use, from L. *usus,* use, a using, service, need, from *utor, usus,* to use (whence also *utility, utensil,* . . . *abuse,* &c.).] The act of employing anything, or the state of being employed; . . . the quality that makes a thing proper for a purpose; . . . continued or repeated practice; wont; usage; . . .

In this reconsideration of my title I find that there are four meanings that I wish to make clear:
(1) The Value of Decoration (Anglice, 'What's the use of it?').
(2) The Appropriateness of it (Anglice, 'Does it fit?').
(3) and (4) Its Practice and Usage (Anglice, 'How it's done' and 'How it works').

Later in these papers I hope to develop and meet the first two questions, here I shall deal specially with practice and usage, and, in the discussion of the craft with which I am most familiar – namely, penmanship – try to show 'how it is done'. No man, however well he knows his craft, can tell another 'how it is done'; he can show to another, by example of his craft, only what that other is able to see – in most cases, a series of unrelated details. No man can know 'how it is done' until he himself has done the thing – and even to that achievement, in its ultimate sense, we can only approach nearer. Let me, therefore,

1. (a) Bamboo Cane ($\frac{1}{8}$-inch nib).
(b) Turkey's Quill ($\frac{1}{16}$-inch nib).

ask the reader who would approach this subject to get or to cut for himself a very broad-nibbed pen – made from a quill, a bamboo cane, or a reed – and, with that in his hand, to follow the argument practically. I subjoin an illustration of the pens with which the following examples were written (1).

Chapter 1   Formal writing and the broad-nibbed pen

By penmanship I mean more particularly that kind of writing in which a broad-nibbed pen is used to form the letters. It is conveniently referred to by the name of 'formal writing', and the early varieties of it are distinguished from the 'running' hands, or ordinary writing, by being called the 'book hands', because for something like 2000 years books were made in such writing, before the invention of printing. In fact, the book as we know it, owes the shapes of its letters and even its familiar form and general plan not to the printers, but to the early scribes or writers of the formal hands. And it is not too much to hope that modern printers and others who are interested in the production and decoration of books – even if they 'cannot do' their writing 'in the old way' – may profit by a study of the methods and principles of that penmanship on which their art is founded.

The three most important things about the broad-nibbed pen, technically considered, are:

(1) That it naturally writes regular thick and thin and graduated strokes, according to its direction (not its pressure).

(2) That the character of its writing depends upon the relative width of the nib in proportion to the height and breadth of the writing, and upon

(3) The direction (or relation to a horizontal line) of the thin edge of the nib.

And here I may add the reminder that the edge of the nib must be kept true and sharp: a blunt pen has its uses for the skilled writer, but, as a tool in the hand of a student of formal writing, it not only damages or blunts the forms of his letters, but hinders or blunts his own apprehension and his constructive faculties.

The fact that a broad-nibbed pen produces thick or thin strokes in absolute relation to its direction, distinguishes it from every other tool and enables it to make, out of collections of simple strokes, letters of marked character and finish with the greatest possible regularity and ease (2,a). Letters such as these, consisting of collections of simple strokes, may correctly be described as 'simple written' forms. Now the simple written letters naturally produced by other tools are generally of the nature of skeleton forms (2,b), and to make letters with the character and finish that are to be obtained by varying the widths of the strokes, the craftsman has to resort to a building-up process, taking a number of strokes – or of such scratches, chippings, stitches, or cuts, as his styles, chisels, needles, gravers, etc., may naturally make – to form one compound stroke (such letters, in which the thick strokes are compound, may be termed 'compound' or 'built-up' letters [2,c]). The pointed pen, or the brush, it is true, in the hand of a skilled writer can simulate the ease and finish of the broad nib, and give us their own equivalent character – in some sort also

29

a 'simple written' letter. The different letter-making tools and their virtues, however, will be discussed later: here we are considering the educative value of the broad-nibbed pen, for those not specially skilled in writing, as the tool that, historically speaking, made our letters for us, and is capable of remaking them now.

**2. (a) Simple written formal writing made with a broad nib.
(b) and (c) Simple skeleton and compound forms made with a pointed tool.[1]**

pen writing
skeleton forms
compound

If our formal writing owes its thick strokes to the 'broad' nib, it follows that the actual width of the nib is of great importance, determining as it does the actual width of our strokes.

'Broad' is, of course, a relative term, and it is the width of our strokes in relation to their height that we must mainly consider. The relative width of the nib, for example, chiefly determines the 'weight' of a letter, and it is obvious that similar letters of the same height (and breadth) will be 'heavy' or 'light' accordingly as they are made with a relatively wide or a relatively narrow nib (3).

3. Examples of heavy and light writing.

formal
formal

The width of the nib in this manner not only determines the weight, but also largely controls the actual forms of the letters (as may be seen by a careful examination of figure 3), so that their character may, in these respects, be said

---

[1] The illustrations are facsimiles in size of their originals, unless specially stated to be reduced or enlarged.

to depend on it. Naturally, the wider the nib, the more it controls the forms, and the more marked becomes their pen character, while the narrower the nib the less marked is the pen character of the letters, and the more is their formation left to the writer's choice and skill. If we take, for example, the following extreme cases, these differences are at once made apparent. Let us write an o and an n in letters $\frac{3}{8}$ inch high with a nib $\frac{1}{8}$ inch wide, and also in letters $1\frac{1}{8}$ inches high with a nib $\frac{1}{16}$ inch wide (4).

4. **Extreme cases of heavy and light writing, showing the domination of the pen in the form and character of the heavy letters.**
$\frac{3}{8}$-inch letters, $\frac{1}{8}$-inch nib.
$1\frac{1}{8}$-inch letters, $\frac{1}{16}$-inch nib.

In these very heavy letters the constructive force and character of the pen are most obvious, but in the lighter letters they are not pronounced, and a greater call is clearly made on the writer's powers of drawing: it may also be seen that the lighter letters are susceptible of a greater variety in their width, and that they might, for example, be made half their present width without loss to their legibility. We may note particularly the remarkable difference in their inside shapes or 'counters', as typefounders call them; the heavy letters showing sudden bends and angles as compared with the smoother curves of the lighter letters. It may also be observed that these heavy letters incline to what is known as the 'Gothic' character, while the lighter letters incline to the 'Roman'. These different effects will be discussed in connexion with different types of letters later on.

It will be found helpful in practice to formulate a rough standard of weight or, rather, to associate our impressions of 'heavy', 'medium' and 'light' letters with approximately corresponding ratios of width of thick strokes to height of letter. In penmanship it is convenient to use the nib of the pen itself as a measure and to express this ratio in nib-widths, which, with the pen held sideways, we may mark alongside the letter (5). Thus we may describe the 'heavy' writing in this example as four nib-widths high, or we may say that the ratio of its nib-width to its letter-height is a quarter.

The terms of weight here suggested for the various ratios are, of course, purely approximate. But I imagine that the normal eye will agree very nearly with this approximation, and also with the suggestion that generally a letter of a height below four-and-a-half nib-widths inclines to be heavy, while one above five-and-a-half nib-widths inclines to be light. I would suggest, further, that the 'extra heavy' writing of three nib-widths high is about the heaviest writing that we may profitably use (except, perhaps, in extraordinary cases); and again, that we should not profitably use a much lighter writing (in ordinary cases) than the 'light' writing of seven nib-widths. It is a good plan for the beginner to write rather heavily – say, with a ratio of 1 : 4, so that the pen will control his hand, and it is also desirable that he should write large – very good proportions are $\frac{1}{2}$-inch writing with an $\frac{1}{8}$-inch pen.

5. Example of letters of various weights of which the ratios are marked in nib widths.

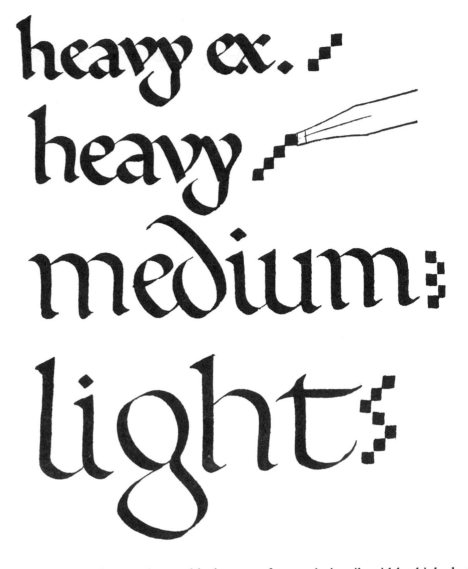

The normal range is roughly between four and six nib-widths high, but great variety is possible within this range, and it is to be observed, in the case of normal letter forms, that a comparatively slight difference in the relative height will make a considerable difference in the apparent weight of the letter, because, ordinarily, it involves a corresponding difference in the breadth of the letter. Thus, a slight increase in the height and in the breadth will make a considerable increase in the total area covered by a letter, and, as the pen strokes – remaining the same width – increase only a very little in their total length, it follows that the greater part of this increase in area will occur in the inside space of the letter (and, moreover, the adjacent spaces – outside the letter – will be affected proportionally). If we compare an n of four nib-widths with an n of five nib-widths (6), we find that, while the latter has an increase

6. An n of four nib-widths and an n of five nib-widths.

in height of only one quarter, and an increase in the total length of its strokes of about one third, its internal space is nearly doubled; and it is obvious that this large increase in the internal space adds greatly to the lightness of the letter. Such enlarged letters, in fact, may be said to be diluted, or reduced in strength, by the greater admixture of background with them.

While in practice their effects cannot well be separated, it will help to clear our conceptions of weight if we distinguish what may be called 'actual weight' from what we may call 'apparent weight'.

The 'actual weight' of a writing, and of its letters, is best expressed by the weight of its strokes, and, as the vertical stroke (or direction of stroke) largely predominates in our letters, we may call the letter i our standard for height and width. In this sense it will be found in practice that the actual weight of a written letter may be very well expressed in the ratio of nib-width to height, as suggested above.

But that effect of weight, which may be distinguished as the 'apparent weight' of a writing, and of its letters, depends rather on the amount of its background, and is best expressed, inversely, by its spaces. In practice we do not measure the letter's actual background, except by the eye, but, occasionally, it will be found of great value to measure in nib-widths the horizontal distance between its strokes. We may take the o as a standard for space. The internal space is of the greatest importance, but the proper background of an o is the whole of the internal and external space which belongs to it, and it may be approximately defined by a parallelogram described about the o, thus (7).

We may say, then, that the 'apparent weight' of a writing, other things being equal, depends on the relation of the total area covered by the pen strokes of the letters, to the total area of their internal and adjacent spaces.

Generally speaking, a 'light letter' has a comparatively large background, and a 'heavy letter' has a comparatively small background: but, as the vertical direction of stroke predominates in our letters, it is obvious that while the 'actual weight' of a writing depends chiefly on the thickness of its strokes, its 'apparent weight' depends chiefly on the distance between the strokes (or the number of strokes to a given space), that is to say, on the breadth of the letter forms in relation to their height.

The normal form of o is approximately circular, and the rest of the small letters follow it closely in their proportions, being also approximately equal in

7. Various o's with their proper backgrounds.

8. Normal and compressed forms.

lighter compressed
writing writing

height and breadth. But there are also distinct narrow and wide types of letters, in which the o, together with the other letters, is compressed or expanded. If we contrast a normal and a compressed form (8) we see how the two writings, written with the same pen and of the same height, differ in apparent weight. Though this compressed writing has a much heavier effect, the 'actual weight' of its letter forms is practically the same as that of the forms in the lighter writing. And as a number of narrow objects standing close together gives an effect of mass, so the apparent weight of the compressed writing is an effect of massing, rather than of actual massiveness. Nevertheless we observe, as a result of the compression, how completely the pen dominates the character of the example given, which, in practice, would properly be called a strong, if not a heavy, writing.

Chapter 2   The development of types, and formal writing

In considering the development of different types of letters, or characters, it is sufficient for our purpose to begin with the Roman capitals from which all our letters are descended. But a brief sketch of the supposed origin of letters may serve not only to show how natural and vital has been their growth, but to strengthen the hands of those who wish to preserve that fine tradition.

The invention of letters, or the development of alphabets [Manuscript annotation by E. J. on printed copy reads: i.e. sets of phonetic signs.] from primitive forms or pictures has, for convenience, been divided into four stages which are called the Mnemonic, the Pictorial, the Ideographic, and the Phonetic. The signs, used in the three later stages, representative of things, ideas, and sounds, respectively, are called 'Pictograms', 'Ideograms', and 'Phonograms'. Among the primitive aids to memory, or Mnemonic symbols, Mr Clodd, in his admirable *Story of the Alphabet* [published by Newnes, 1900. Out of print. *Ed.*] refers to the knotted strings or Quipu of the ancient Peruvians. By means of these, it is said, they not only registered details of the army or of their treasures of gold and silver or of corn, but actually kept the annals of their Empire and 'set down' its laws. Mr Clodd also refers to 'the knot which we tie in our handkerchief' at the present day. Countless examples of the later signs have been discovered in both the Old World and the New, and in both a similar, though probably an entirely independent, development appears to have taken place. Mr Clodd quotes, for example, from Mercer's *Hill Caves of Yucatan*, 'The Mayas [of ancient Mexico], like the Egyptians, had proceeded beyond pictures to hieroglyphs, where symbols, more or less arbitrary, stand for words or syllables, and the mind prepares itself to invent an alphabet.'

This remote and marvellous development we may faintly image thus: if, by a flight of imagination, we suppose ourselves to be primitive and without letters, it is probable that our artists would, sooner or later, produce an approximate circle as a symbol or pictogram of the SUN. Then, in time, having become used to this and to kindred symbols and to purely pictorial records, we should go a step further, and the circle might be made to stand for the ideograph of LIGHT. Finally – by a process resembling punning – the circle might come to be a phonogram for the sound Li or L, and we should at length have achieved a letter of the alphabet.

It may easily be seen how our apparently arbitrary Letter Forms are really economic simplifications of early pictograms: let us take two actual examples. In our letter M we can still discern the face of the OWL that was used by the Egyptians in their hieroglyphic phonogram for M thousands of years ago. In a monument assigned to about 4000 BC (preserved in the Ashmolean Museum

35

at Oxford) and described by Mr Falconer Madan [in *Books in Manuscript*, pub. Kegan Paul, 1893. Out of print. *Ed.*] as probably the oldest (surviving) piece of writing in the world, the name of SEND, 'a king of the second dynasty', is actually written alphabetically. We can even recognize the features of our own letter forms in these distant relatives (9).

9. The earliest (Phonographic) writing extant, and its phonetic value.

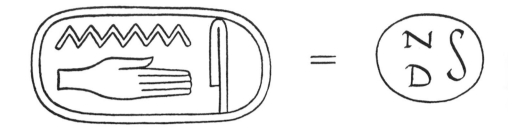

Of the known ancestry of our own letters, that is, of the ROMAN CAPITALS – an alphabet about 2500 years old – Sir Edward Maunde Thompson says, 'The alphabet which we use at the present day . . . is directly derived from the Roman alphabet; the Roman from a local form of the Greek; the Greek, from the Phœnician . . .'. It had long been supposed that the Phœnician came from the Egyptian hieratic, but 'Recent discoveries prove the existence, in very remote times, in all quarters of the Mediterranean and in Egypt, of symbols resembling certain alphabetical signs and preceding even the Egyptian hieroglyphics. The early origin of our alphabet therefore still remains to be worked out' (*Greek and Latin Palæography*, 3rd edition, 1906, pp.1, 321).

Judging by the examples extant, the earliest Roman capitals were somewhat roughly formed and without thick and thin strokes. But the growth of the custom of cutting monumental inscriptions in stone led to a highly developed form in the first century BC. These later inscriptions are said to have been carefully outlined or painted – commonly in red-lead – before they were cut (and often to have been painted in the same colour after they were cut). Such inscriptional forms reached their highest development in the first and second

10. Outline sketch of letters from the Trajan Column inscription. Scale one-sixth original height.

centuries AD. One of the finest examples is that of the inscription on the Trajan Column of about AD 114 (10). The cast of this (No.1864–128) in the South Kensington Museum is worth studying. It will be seen that the strokes in this inscription vary in thickness (though not with absolute regularity) accordingly as they are vertical, horizontal, oblique, or curved, and that the curves are 'tilted'. Now, as this variety does not appear to come from anything in the stone and chisel themselves, or from methods peculiar to their use, we must look somewhere else for a cause. And as all these effects are necessarily produced by a broad-nibbed pen held at a natural slant (11), it is reasonable to

11. Characterization of skeleton capitals by a broad-nibbed pen.

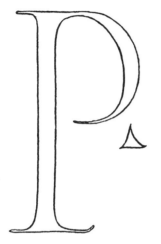

12. Letter (traced from Hubner's Exempla, No.149) from Puteoli, incised early in the first century AD (Scale one-fifth original height).

suppose that the use of the pen may have strongly influenced the finished Roman characters.

The careful carving of inscriptions in stone led, no doubt, to a formal type, and possibly to the curving out of the stems, which, carried on into the 'serifs', gave an effect of great elegance to the letter. An almost exaggerated example of this is given in figure 12. But it will be observed that this earlier example also strongly supports the argument in favour of the pen's influence.

The letters of the earliest Latin Formal MSS naturally have a strong resemblance to the letters of the monumental inscriptions. They differ chiefly in this, that whereas the letters in stone are built-up or compound forms, the MS letters are simple-written, and the varying widths of their strokes are in absolute relation to the breadth and direction of the nib.

It has been stated in Chapter 1 that the character of the broad-nibbed pen's writing depends partly on 'the direction (or relation to a horizontal line) of the thin edge of the nib'. This will be discussed further in the next chapter in connexion with the later MS forms, but it is well to realize at once the striking effects that changing the nib's direction produced in the development of types. Broadly speaking, we may hold the pen straight or slanted (13,a,b); or

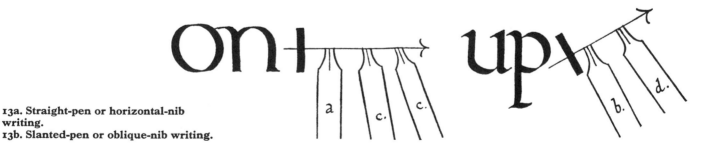

13a. Straight-pen or horizontal-nib writing.
13b. Slanted-pen or oblique-nib writing.

– what is more usual – we may alter the direction of the nib's edge by cutting at different angles to the shaft (13,c,d). For many years I have called the mode of writing that produces a horizontal thin line, 'straight pen' writing, and the mode that produces an oblique thin line, 'slanted pen' writing. Though these terms are convenient, when they are understood, I propose in future to use the more explicit terms 'Horizontal-nib' writing and 'Oblique-nib' writing.

The chief differences to be observed in the effects of these two modes are the following:

The Horizontal-nib naturally produces a comparatively slow, round, formal, upright, and elegant letter, having a forward movement.

The Oblique-nib tends to produce a comparatively rapid, angular, compressed, heavy-shouldered, and strong letter, having an up and down movement. (This letter is apt to lose its pure form and, accordingly as the scribe is over careful or careless, to become more ornamental or less formal.)

In practice all formal writing shows the use of a more or less oblique-nib, though some of the most remarkable MSS show a thin stroke so nearly horizontal that we are justified in calling them horizontal-nib writings; indeed, if we attempt to imitate these MSS we actually find it necessary to pretend that the nib is horizontal. The natural conclusion that it is easier to write with an oblique-nib, may be immediately confirmed by a few minutes' practice, and we shall find it is borne out by the history of formal writing wherein both the primitive and the advanced stages are marked by its use. [Manuscript annotation by E.J. on printed copy reads: Footnote (i.e. the stages of *early effort* and *later haste*). The round h.n. MS are to be found in the n'brhood of the 7th century. (e.g. Book of Kells) & Represent an economic degradation of this flowering.][1]

R.CAPITALS SQ.CAPITALS

14. Rustic Capitals. Square Capitals.

The earliest, most formal, Latin MSS surviving are assigned approximately to the fourth century; their letters are known as 'Square Capitals' and 'Rustic Capitals' (14). In the former the obliqueness of the nib is rather less than in the latter, while, in both, the nib-direction is subject to considerable variation – which indicates a slightly artificial, though quite legitimate mode. Though writing of a less formal sort, in the style of the Rustic Capitals, is found in the earliest extant Latin MSS, and the earliest known MS in Square Capitals is ascribed to the end of the fourth century, yet there is reason to suppose that the Square form (as it did in the stone inscriptions) possibly preceded the Rustic form. The latter – being written with a more slanted pen – may very well have been a more easily written pen development of the former.

Books do not appear to have been written in either of these hands after the close of the fifth century, though the Square, to some extent, and, most notably, the Rustic Capitals survived in ornamental titles, and the like, for many centuries. The survival of the Rustic letter may indeed be compared with the present survival of 'black letter' for ornamental purposes: it is a testimony to the greater ease of writing it and to its ornamental qualities, which might justify the revival of the Rustic character for occasional use (this will be referred to later, in connexion with ornamental writing).

[1] The position of this footnote on the page suggests that it refers to the latter part of para. 4, but it could refer to para. 3. *Ed.*

Chapter 3   The development of types, and formal writing (continued)

In Chapter 2 reference was made to our ancestral type – the Roman Capital – being about 2500 years old, and it was shown that about the beginning of the Christian era the inscriptional form was fully developed and the formal manuscript was merely a pen-made variety of the capital.

We must leave the pen, for a moment, to consider the effect on this development of another tool, namely the stylus. While a careful formal letter on papyrus (which became still more finished on the introduction of vellum) was used by the scribes for a book-hand (that is to say, for the making of books), the ordinary writing of the people consisted generally of skeleton capitals (15, 2) rapidly scratched by means of a metal or ivory stylus on wooden tablets coated with black wax. In this process the Roman capitals inevitably underwent an economic development, having their strokes reduced in number or otherwise simplified: this is indicated diagrammatically in figure 16 on page 42.

It is worth noting that two letters, at least (A and B), had two quite separate developments that eventually appear to have merged, in each case, in one form (a and b); the two 'a' forms, if they did not actually merge, were, at any rate, at one time very closely related. The forms in the second development of b are known to have occurred, but as I have no facsimiles to copy them from I have put them in the figure in round brackets. The forms shown, not in brackets, are taken from Maunde Thompson's *Greek and Latin Palæography*. It is also noted that we can still trace the ancestral capital form in the features of our small letters and that there appears reason to suspect that the Roman capitals have always made their dominant influence felt by their wayward descendants. B and b, for example, are most obviously related and yet by the first development of b the stem seems to have stood for the bows, and the bow for the stem, of its ancestor. Note: the letters c, f, i, l, o, p, s, x have suffered little or no change: the letters j, m, n, q, t are also quite simple developments from the original capitals.

We see how greatly the stylus affected the development of our letter forms, and, though it made only skeleton forms, its effects (coupled no doubt with the individuality of its users) were sufficiently remarkable to have given us the word 'style' (implying fashion) which is directly derived from it. Let us remember, then, in relation to decoration, that any naturally handled tool will inevitably produce its natural or proper effects.

The table of developments (page 40), and the graphic illustration of them in figure 15, will repay study, though they are intended here rather for purposes of reference. In the next chapter the development of types will be concluded and the choice of letter forms, and the simple arrangement of letters, will be considered.

Table of derivations and approximate periods of the Roman derivatives (v. figure 15 opposite) mainly compiled from Maunde Thompson's *Greek and Latin Palæography*.

Derivation	Name	Approximate period of development & use (numerals mean centuries, — before, + after)	Notes	Reference numbers in figure 15
From Greek	Roman Capitals	About 600 BC to present day		1
(Stylus varieties)	Roman Cursive	—1st AD to (?) 6th century	There is also a Literary (pen) cursive about 5th–7th century, and an inferior form which lasted till the 13th century	2
(Pen varieties)	Roman Sq. Caps Roman Rustic Caps	(?—1st) to 5th century —1st to 5th century	used later for special lettering (see p. 38)	3 3a
From Capitals & Cursive (influenced by Greek Uncials?)	Roman Uncials	(2nd to 4th) 5th to 8th century		4
From Cursive & Uncials	Roman Half-Uncials	5th to 6th century		5
From Roman Half-Uncials	Irish Half-Uncials	+ 7th to 8th century		6
From Irish Half-Uncials	English Half-Uncials	About AD 634 to AD 840		7
From Roman Cursive	Merovingian (French) Visigothic (Spanish) Lombardic (Italian)	7th to 9th century (?)— 8th to 12th century —9th to 13th century		8 8a
From Merovingian, Roman Half-Uncial & English influence	Caroline reform (Caroline or Carlovingian writing)	About —AD 796 to +AD 804	In France, especially at Tours under Alcuin of York. The Caroline hands which spread over Europe, established themselves in England in the 10th century (Reference No.10)	9
From earlier native hands, through the Caroline reformed hands	Compressed, angular hands of N. Europe Open (round) Italian hands	—12th to 15th century 11th, 12th and 15th century	Note: The 15th century Italian hands were directly modelled on their native 11th & 12th century hands by the scribes of the Renaissance	11 & 12 11a & 12a
From compressed angular hands (above)	'Black letter' or 'Gothic' types	About AD 1455 to present day		
From Italian Renaissance hands (above)	'Roman' small letter types	(1465), AD 1470 to present day		
From Manuscript forms	'Italic' types	AD 1501 to present day		

40

15. Examples of Roman derivatives freely copied from photographs (1 reduced; 2–12 approx. original size) Note: 3–12a are all written with a broad-nibbed pen.

(1) Epitaph inscribed slab (Rome) about 250 BC

SCIPIONE·FILIOS

(2) Wax tablet (Dacia) 17 March, AD 139

MAXIMVS DATIVS (= MAXIMVS BATONIS)

(3) 4th–5th C Virgil
(3a) 3rd–4th C Virgil

DICTOPARENS   INTERPRIMOS

(4) 5th century psalter

CUSTODIAM

(5) 6th century

extra ecclesiam

(6) 'Book of Kells', 7th century

multos aegros

(7) 'Durham Book', about AD 700[1]

Sciteuim pater uester

(8) AD 744, St Jerome
(8a) about AD 1070 Lectionary

lamentationem   laruat nos

(9) early 9th century

tantae rei miraculo. idquod ipsa

(10) probably Winchester late 10th century[2]

benedicite stellae celi dno

(11) Winchester Bible about AD 1170
(11a) first half 12th C

habebatq: gratis plurimos   annorum nonaginta

(12) 15th century
(12a) 15th century

Et bien + pais loyautez.   animus fallit · gratissimum

[1] [Lindisfarne Gospels. BM. MS Cotton Nero D. iv. *Ed.*]
[2] [The Ramsey Psalter. BM, Harley MS 2904. *Ed.*]

41

16. The centre column shows the process of development of the Roman capital into Roman small letters. Most of the forms shown were scratched with a stylus in the first and second centuries AD, but the last (lower) a, (upper) b, d, (upper) g, r, and u are cursive pen forms of the sixth century. The forms shown in square brackets are conjectural links.

Chapter 4 The development of types, and formal writing (continued)

The development of types is here concluded by four figures (17–20) illustrating the letter forms used by the first printers. These figures are reproduced by permission of the British Museum authorities from the official 'Guide to the Exhibition in the King's Library, illustrating the History of Printing, Music-printing and Book-binding' (1901, price sixpence).[1] A visit to the British Museum will convince the receptively minded of the fine quality of these early works. Such technical flaws as may be found in them by a modern critic are far out-weighed by the breadth of their conception and their simple magnificence, to which our blocks at secondhand do but scant justice.

The early printers have been accused of 'imitating' the style of the manuscript books. It is to be remembered that, while we think of books as printed books, to the first printers, and their public, books were written books – the work and traditional production of the penman. The normal attitude of mind towards any craft or art is worthy of attention: while our friends, for example, compliment us who are trying to revive the book-hands, or formal writings, by saying 'How beautifully you print', doubtless it is by a corresponding confusion of thought that some antiquarians have been led to accuse the early printers of making imitation MSS. The common processes of thought necessarily refer to the new in terms of the old, but, while acknowledging this necessity, we should endeavour to keep our minds clear and unconfused and receptive to the true nature of things. I cannot attempt to do justice to the overwhelming importance – especially to would-be decorators – of the question of what a thing *is*, but I shall refer to it at every opportunity and try to show that it is the first concern of every man.

The first printers' types were naturally and inevitably the more formalized, or materialized, letters of the writer. The likeness of the type in the earliest book (17) to the French MSS of the fifteenth century shown in Chapter 3 (15, No.12) is very clear.

We may now cast our eye over the first 2000 years of our Roman letter's development: we find its beginning in a skeleton alphabet (derived from Greek forms) and then occurs, on the one hand, a formal characterization of this alphabet (carved or written by craftsmen) influenced and largely produced by the broad-nibbed pen, and, on the other hand, a less formal characterization resulting from the scribbling of the educated public: this development at first controlled by the tool and material – the stylus and wax tablets of the public – was mastered by them, the 'scribblers', and became an economic development, simplified strokes, and linkings or loopings, saving both time and space. The craftsmen in their turn, borrowing these more economic skeleton forms, characterized them afresh by means of the broad nib, and, in the medieval

[1] This admirable little guide has thirty-six illustrations, with notes on the famous printers: it should be in the hands of every printer who loves his craft (a new edition of it is, I understand, on the eve of publication). [Now out of print. *Ed.*]

17. Mainz, not later than 1456, part of a column of the forty-two line Bible.

septem diebus et septem noctibus: et nemo loquebatur ei verbum. Videbant enim dolorem esse vehementem. III Post hec aperuit iob os suum: et maledixit diei suo: & locutus est. Pereat dies in qua natus sum: et nox in qua dictum est conceptus est homo. Dies illa vertetur in tenebras. Non requirat eum deus desuper et non illustret lumine. Obscurent eum tenebre & umbra mortis. Occupet eum caligo & involuatur amaritudine. Noctem illam tenebrosus turbo possideat. Non computetur in diebus anni nec numeretur in mensibus. Sit nox illa solitaria: nec

18. Subiaco, Sweynheym and Pannartz, 1465, part of page of 'Lactantius'.

Eclarauit ut opinor animam non esse solubilem. superest citare testes quorum autoritate argumeta firment. Neqz nuc prophetas in testimoim uocabo. quoy ratio et diuinatio in hoc solo posita est: ut ad cultum dei et ad imortalitate ab eo accipienda creari homine doceant. sed eos pocius qbus istos qui respuut ueritate credere sit necesse. Hermes naturam describes ut doceret qademodum esser a deo factus hec intulit. και αυτο εξ εκατε. ρων φυσεων της τε αθαματον και της θρητης μιαν επο ιει φυσιν αμθρωπουτον αυτον πη μεν αθαματον πη δε θρητον ποιησας και τουτον φερων εν μεσω θειας και αβαματον φυσεως και της θρητης και ευμεταβλητου ιδρυσεν ιρα ορων απαρτα απαρτα καιθαυμαση. Id est. Et idem ex utraqz natura mortali et immortali unam faciebat naturam hois: eundem in aliquo qdem imortalem in aliquo aute mortale faciens: et hunc ferens in medio diuine et immortalis nature. et mortalis mutabilisqz constituit. ut omnia uidens omnia miret. Sed hunc fortasse aliquis in numero

19. Venice, Jenson, 1471, Colophon of 'Decor Puellarum', misdated 1461.

io in alcuna cofla haueffe p ignorãtia
o per inaduertentia manchato trãffor·
mato:ouer incompofitamente,pferto
ueramente rechiedo perdono fempre
fopponendoui ad ogni fpirituale &
temporale correctione de qualunque
diuotiffima perfona di zafchaduno
perito maeftro & fapientiffio doctore
de la uoftra factiffima madre ecclefia
catholica di roma.

ANNO A CHRISTI INCARNA·
TIONE.MCCCCLXI.PER MAGI·
STRVM NICOLAVM IENSON
HOC OPVS QVOD PVELLA·
RVM DECOR DICITVR FELICI·
TER IMPRESSVM EST.

LAVS DEO.

writings, achieved characters of unequalled clearness and beauty. Having reached this summit of perfection the professional tended to degenerate, the development of formal writing becoming firstly economic, by a more rapid style and by compression and reduction, and, secondly, ornamental, by an over development of the details of form, and the combination of writing with ornament that is familiarly known as illumination. At the critical moment the early printers appeared upon the scene, and the importance of the letter-form and of readableness again became predominant. No doubt the history of printing will receive attention in future numbers of *The Imprint*: it is sufficient for us to note the high quality of the first printers who based their types on writing.

It is interesting to note in passing how each nation played its part. The Romans – who obtained their alphabet from the Greeks – passed on their best hands to Ireland; the Irish, perfecting these, passed them on to England, and the English hand is thought to have influenced the reformed hands in France. The French gave these hands to the rest of Europe, and the Italians finally gave the world the small 'roman' and 'italic' forms. The first printers were Germans.

I have dwelt on this matter because we see in brief in the development of types how natural was their growth: a growth more natural in writing than in any other craft – if we may call anything more natural than another – because, in its essence, it was more subservient to its purpose, more rapid, and less thought out. A well-known designer once said to me, 'You scribes are the fellows, you don't have to think at all'. This is true in its best sense, and the

20. Venice, Aldus, 1501, page from the Virgil printed in Italics.

P.O.N·IN PRIMVM GEORGICORVM,
ARGVMENTVM·

Quid faciat lætas segetes,quæ sydera seruet
Agricola,ut facilem terram proscindat aratris,
Semina quo iacienda modo, cultus'q; locorum
E docuit, messes magno olim fœnore reddi.

P.V·M·GEORGICORVM LIBER PRI
MVS AD MOECENATEM·

           Vid faciat lætas segetes,quo sydere
            terram,
q   Vertere Mœcenas,ulmis'q; adiun
           gere uites,
           Conueniat,quæ cura boum,quis
           cultus habendo
Sit pecori,atq; apibus quanta experientia parcis,
Hinc canere incipiam. Vos o clarissima mundi
Lumina,labentem cœlo quæ ducitis annum
Liber,et almā Ceres,uestro si munere tellus
Chaoniam pingui glandem mutauit arista,
Poculaq; inuentis Acheloia miscuit uuis,
Et uos agrestum præsentia numina Fauni,
Ferte simul,Fauniq; pedem,Dryades'q; puellæ,
Munera uestra cano,tu'q; o cui prima frementem
Fudit equum magno tellus percussa tridenti
Neptune,et cultor nemorum,cui pinguia Cææ
Ter centum niuei tondent dumeta iuuenci,
Ipse nemus liquens patrium,saltus'q; Licæi
                      c

first lesson I would draw from penmanship, for the consideration of decorators, is that natural growth should take the first place in their work, for conscious design is only tolerable when it is the act of one thus set free, of one to whom the right thing comes naturally because his work has grown naturally.

46

Chapter 5   The choice of letter forms and the simple arrangement of letters

Instinctive choice is the decorator's soundest guide: if it be encouraged it will bring us unscathed through all the theories – even through the theories that we ourselves create. But our instincts have been so much disused or abused that reason must be called to our aid. How many, in these days, who are interested in decoration know what they really like? It is no passing fancy or doubtful attraction, but it is that which we really like, that matters, and that ought to triumph at last over all materialistic systems and rules. Let us then honestly try to find out what we really like, and – in the meantime – endeavour to be reasonable.

Now if we are to choose letter forms, the only reasonable course open to us is to do so on the basis of readableness. We will, however, make our basis as wide as possible; we therefore take readableness to imply not only easy-to-read but pleasant-to-read. If, for the sake of clearness, we here distinguish these qualities, we may also say that, while it is the general function of the craftsman to make a thing legible, it is his particular function as a decorator to make it becoming.

We have discovered then that one of the uses of decoration is to make a thing pleasant to read; but, unless the decorator – like the poet – is 'born', he must begin at the beginning and deal first with the more practical side of readableness, that is, with legibility.

There are three things which constitute legibility, namely, simplicity, distinctiveness, proportion. Besides these abstract qualities there are various concrete aspects of legibility; the two most important are accustomedness and fitness. We do not require new forms – in this sense, 'that which is new is not true' – but, though we may hope to better their character, we must accept the symbols of present use. Our current letters – whether of printing, or of common writing, or however made – are the ROMAN CAPITAL, the Roman small-letter, and the *italic*; and it is with these three forms that we must ordinarily deal, regarding ornamental and other forms as departures from the standard, and therefore as marked for occasional use. Fitness, that is the suitability or adaptableness for a given purpose, will be considered in connexion with special cases.

The broad-nibbed pen will create for us a standard of its own, not a departure from the current standard, but a variety, just as the printer's types – though they seem nearly to fill the whole field of vision – are themselves a variety (or varieties). I give here (21) a reasonably representative version of this pen standard. The pen standard, which with a little care we can all of us recreate, has the peculiar virtue – as far as the small-letters are concerned – of being essentially the ancestral type (so that, literally, all other varieties are

ABCDEFGHIJKLMNOPQRSTUVWXYZ Skeltns.

PEN:ABCDHIJMOR

abcdefghijklmnopqrstuvwxyz "roman" small-letter Skeletons.

pen·abcdfghijklmoqrstuv

xyz "rom". foundational han

abcdefghijklmnopqrstuvwxyz italic skeletons

pen·abcdefghijklmoqrstuvwxyz

21. Skeletons of the current standard forms and a suggested pen standard (in oblique-nib writing). Note: The natural pen hooks and strokes are here used for terminals or serifs.

varieties of it). The example of it is given here in the hope that decorators may acquire it, or a similar formal hand. Having such hands at our command, we may experiment freely in form and arrangement of letters, and it is certain that most of us can in this way discover the 'theory and practice' of decoration more easily and surely than by any other means.

Simple written Roman Capitals. It will be remembered that certain early MSS were written entirely in capitals (15, Nos.3, 3a), but when the new manner of writing in 'small-letters' (15, No.5) came into use it was regarded *as a different writing*, complete in itself. The Roman capital survived in the shape of important initials and in headings, etc., but we do not find it written to match the small-letter writing of the medieval MSS. Nevertheless we can make it for ourselves, by using the same pen, held in the same manner, as we use for the small letters. For example, the capitals given in figure 21 are simply what the pen makes of the ordinary abstract or skeleton forms (compare 11, chapter 2). Similarly – among the varied forms of the Roman capital – we can take *round* (or 'branch-topped') and *flourished* capitals and characterize them with the pen (22).

Roman small-letters. The MS example in figure 21 (q.v.) is made from the skeleton small-letters which are given there; but, in effect, it is nearly identical with the ancestral tenth-century MS given in figure 15 (No.10). By using a narrower nib, and by making stroke terminals, a still more 'Roman' hand can be made from this (23).

Italics. The MS example in figure 21 (q.v.), though based on the skeleton italic which is given there, is derived directly from the foundational hand above

BDDEFHM PRTUW Round or Branch-Topped Romans

BDDEFHMPRTUW

AABBDDEEFF GHJLMMNRRTVW Flourished Romans

AABBEEFGILMRT

abcdefghijklmnpqrstuvx

22 (top). 'Branch-topped' and flourished roman capitals made with a pen. 23 (above). A more 'Roman' development from the pen standard, or 'foundational', hand.

it (by compression, elongation of *ascenders* and *descenders*, and slight sloping). It can also be made more 'Roman' by the use of a narrower nib.

It is to be observed that from this pen standard small-letter of figure 21, which I call the 'foundational hand', various more 'Roman' forms may be derived, and also various italic forms; and we will find that, by using a broader nib, we can also make of it a more 'Gothic' character (see figure 4 and pp. 31 and 32), and can develop a 'black letter' variety (24). Besides being useful in itself, particularly as an educational hand, it forms therefore an excellent general basis for further development, and I would strongly recommend its acquisition by craftsmen generally. It may be noted here that, other things being equal, the open hands are more legible than the compressed, and the forms of medium weight are more legible than the heavy forms. The most legible hand will probably be found to have an externally circular o, and a stroke-weight of about one-fifth its height.

For the general 'qualities of good writing' I shall at present refer the reader to the section and the table – under that name – in my handbook[1] in the 'Artistic Crafts Series'. But the three abstract qualities referred to above as constituting legibility may be graphically illustrated here, thus:

Simplicity: that is, *having only necessary parts* (25, I).

Distinctiveness: that is, *having marked features* (25, II).

Proportion: that is, *having each part of its proper value* (25, III).

I have in this example designedly chosen a quite passable (modern) 'black-letter' capital, as a foil, to illustrate in the abstract the nature of legibility. If it were desirable for this purpose to exhibit 'horrid examples', how many of our

[1] *Writing & Illuminating, & Lettering*, 4th edn., 1911 (John Hogg, 6s. 6d.) [Out of date. Now published by Sir Isaac Pitman & Sons. *Ed.*]

49

24. 'Gothic' and 'black-letter' developments of the 'foundational' hand.

ordinary 'display' types could be refused a dishonourable place? Perfect legibility is sometimes not necessary and, occasionally, even undesirable: but a departure from the legible standard requires a reason or, in other words, a compensation, to justify it. For example, the value of 'black-letter' (both capital and small-letter) as an occasional form, is largely due to the fact that, without an increase in 'actual weight', it will give an increase in 'apparent weight', by which we may obtain a vivid contrast with our ordinary Roman type.

We can thus state in a general way the qualities and features that should be sought when we aim at ordinary legibility, and for general purposes the 'foundational' and related hands given above fulfil the conditions. But, for special purposes, we make – or, more correctly, the circumstances themselves make – special developments which give the particular quality of fitness.

For those who wish to take up formal writing more thoroughly, a course of practice in the 'straight-nib' forms helps to form the hand (and, I think, the judgement too). The simplified 'half-uncial' of figure 26 is very good for this purpose. The characteristic difference between this and the 'foundational hand' will be appreciated best by practical experiment: reference may be made to the comparison of 'straight-nib' writing with 'oblique-nib' writing in pages 37 and 38, Chapter 2.

Using our standard hands as 'counters' we can now proceed to the question of the simple arrangement of letters. It will be found that all the previous remarks on readableness of form apply equally to arrangement: so that legibility also requires a

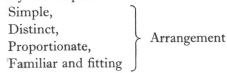

Simple,
Distinct,
Proportionate,
Familiar and fitting   } Arrangement

The familiar arrangement of letters is the placing of a number of lines in a rectangular space. But we can simplify our conceptions of arrangement if we put the matter thus:

In general the treatment of lettering is the treatment of LINES of letters.

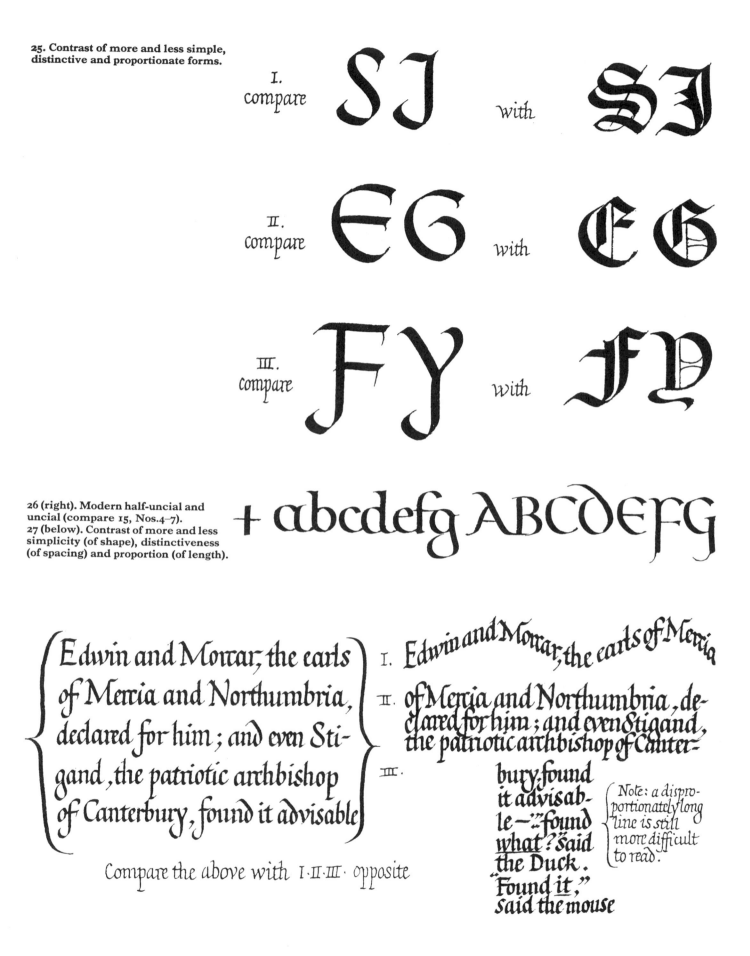

25. Contrast of more and less simple, distinctive and proportionate forms.

I. compare **SJ** with **SJ**

II. compare **EG** with **EG**

III. compare **FY** with **FY**

26 (right). Modern half-uncial and uncial (compare 15, Nos.4–7).
27 (below). Contrast of more and less simplicity (of shape), distinctiveness (of spacing) and proportion (of length).

+ abcdefg ABCDEFG

{ Edwin and Morcar, the earls of Mercia and Northumbria, declared for him; and even Stigand, the patriotic archbishop of Canterbury, found it advisable }

I. Edwin and Morcar, the earls of Mercia

II. of Mercia and Northumbria, declared for him; and even Stigand, the patriotic archbishop of Canterbury,

III. bury, found it advisable—"found what? said the Duck. "Found it," said the mouse

Note: a disproportionately long line is still more difficult to read.

Compare the above with I·II·III· opposite

D ignare dñe die isto:
sine peccato nos custodire ·
M iserere nri dñe. miserere nri ·
F iat misericordia tua dñe
sup nos. quem admodum
sperauimus inte   ·:   ·:
I nte dñe speraui. nonconfun
dar inadernum   ·:   ·:

HYMNUS TRIUM PUERORUM.
B enedicite omña opera dñi dño ·
laudate & super exaltate
eum insecula · ·:   ·:   ·:
B eñ angeli dñi dño. b celi dño   ·:
B eñ aquae omñs quae sup celos
sunt dño. b omñs uirtutes dñi dño ·:
B eñ sol & luna dño
benedicite stellae celi dño · ·:   ·:
B eñ omñs imber & ros dño ·:

28 (left). Page of MS psalter of the tenth century, probably written at Winchester. [The Ramsey Psalter. BM, Harley MS 2904. Now thought to have been written at Ramsey in Huntingdonshire. Ed.]

Therefore, in general the line is a much more important unit than the page. Some applications of the abstract qualities in the treatment of lines may be graphically illustrated thus (27).

Again we note that the contrasted modes on the right of this figure are quite legitimate in their proper places, and, like the less legible forms of figure 25, have a certain decorative value to commend them. But we are trying to discover a common standard, and these, more ornamental varieties are clearly departures from our standard – suitable, maybe, on occasion, but requiring a reason or compensation to justify their use.

Among the phenomena of familiarity we may note that by use our eye is trained to accept the vertical rules of newspaper columns in lieu of margins, so that we generally remain blind to the contents of the neighbouring columns. Fitness of arrangement, as before mentioned, is the development for – or, more properly, by – a special use.

Chapter 6   Special arrangement of letters–the book

The reiterated statement of the last chapter must again be quoted: 'Fitness [of form or arrangement] is the development for – or, more properly, by – a special use.' A special use implies a special object or thing. Now I must ask the reader's patience if – attempting a task which is as greatly difficult as it is supremely important – I labour the point of this.

If we intend to make some thing, the clearest conception possible of *what that thing is* is our first concern; for that which it is indeed is the realization of our intention. I say the clearest conception possible, because it is doubtful whether a man can be quite clear as to what he intends until he has done his work; but to achieve reality it is essential that we have a measure of clearness in our intention.

It may be said of a man working vaguely, that, setting out to make a chair he finds he has made a table – by mistake. This accident is not peculiar to *carpenters*, indeed carpenters are less prone to it than most people, because their stuffs and their tools so often carry them through. Perhaps we may hazard the guess that the *artist* and the *legislator* vie with each other in producing the greatest number of accidental effects; but no man is free of this fault, for in fact every man is an artist and a legislator, let him deny it with his tongue if he please.

Strictly speaking, human success is a happy accident: but that half-god, Luck – whom we think so well of that it is common to wish a man 'goodbye and good luck' (Good b'ye seemingly having lost its original meaning) – that luck so vitally helpful as it is, so strangely unaccountable, may at times not only lead us but be persuaded to follow; for if we ourselves follow right ways, happy accidents become a habit. The right way to set about making a chair is to intend 'chair' with all our will; our old friends simplicity, distinctiveness, proportion come to our aid, and, if we are happy, the chair – legible, or at least recognizable – will be achieved.

I think it will be admitted that clearness of intention, though related to definiteness, bears a finer sense, as of something made visible and shining rather than something limited and outlined. And it is desirable to point out that such clearness of intention does not necessitate great planning or scheming, and that over-planning is one of the greatest dangers we have to beware of. Its speciousness misleads the practical: it is far worse than under-planning – the 'chair' of the mere dreamer may be passable, but the chair (or sofa) of the schemer, we have been told, was convertible into a table or a step-ladder. Thus the schemer achieves confusion, and, over-reaching himself, falls into much deeper error than the witless. This applies alike to the humblest works and to the greatest; between a chair and a cathedral there is only a difference of

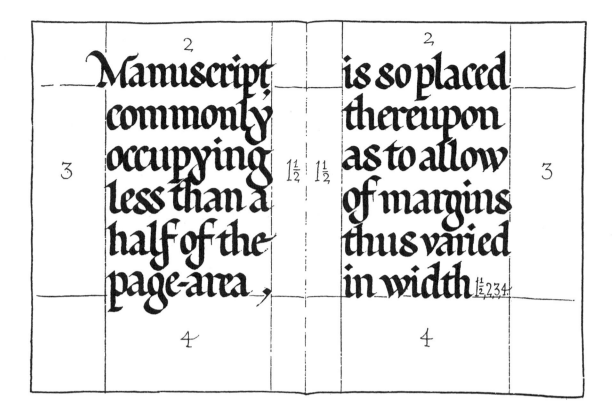

29. Arrangement or plan of the 'opening' in a medieval book.

degree, the table and the tavern are relations; the 'workman' whose 'chair', by lack of meaning, becomes a 'table', or the 'architect', whose 'cathedral' becomes a 'tavern', does less harm than the schemer whose 'cathedral' will have a *barber's shop* and a *crematorium* attached to it (*and shops on the ground floor to pay the rent*).

The objection to over-planning applies to all pre-designing – which, in its tendency to suppress natural growth in the working, forms the almost insuperable difficulty of the professional 'designer' who is not a craftsman, and is the acknowledged solicitude of all good architects who are not builders. The remedy is to know what we are aiming at and, at the same time, to allow our work to grow naturally. This apparent paradox is not self-contradictory, as the work of the early craftsmen proves for us and as we, in our work, may prove again. Man's general aim in respect of his work may be hinted at – *to do his work well* is probably near the mark. Beauty – in its finest sense perhaps the ultimate aim – is more truly a divine reward than his direct objective. Thus I would attempt to plead with decorators who desire something finer than the riot of 'display' decoration – as we may call it – of the modern world, to seek for simplicity in their intentions together with clearness; then, if our methods are right, the work will grow by nature beautiful.

What then are right methods? Here is the practical problem of every man's craft. We can only speak generally – natural growth implies natural and workmanlike methods, that is to say, the methods of tradition or the methods developed by the work itself. In the treatment of special examples I shall endeavour to show – as far as it is possible in these papers – how these methods may be followed, and also how proper methods may be evolved.

For our first special example we will take the book – a subject which I can only introduce in this chapter, and hope in the next to develop in some detail. The book, as we know it, consists of a number of leaves hinged together at one side. Its treatment differs from that of the broadside or panel inscription (which is like a single page) chiefly in this, that the several pages of the book being numerous and – inasmuch as they are bound at one side and free at the other – not symmetrical, we may take as many pages as we want, not having to fit our text to one given page, but continually turning over a new leaf, and we also treat the several pages – in relation to their binding – asymmetrically. Symmetry of text and margin is, of course, the general rule in the 'opening' of the book, that is, in its opposite pages taken together. The book is also *portable*, and therefore it is not so dependent on its surroundings as a panel or wall-inscription is.

The approximate proportions and arrangement of the opening of a medieval book are indicated diagrammatically in figure 29.

Chapter 7 Special arrangement of letters – the book (continued)

It is now to be shown in the making of a manuscript book – the exemplar of the printed book – how 'natural and workmanlike methods' are followed and are 'developed by the work itself'.

The first considerations are the nature and use of the book: these demand a suitable treatment of its subject matter and an accustomed and fitting shape for its purpose. Its treatment therefore follows tradition and custom – in so far as they are natural and healthy – rather than extravagant design.

Generally the size of the book is first settled; that is, the size and shape of its leaves are determined approximately. And though, in deciding whether a book shall be 'large' or 'small' or of medium size, we are naturally influenced by the subject matter, *use* is the chief guide; and it is things such as these that the right craftsman bears in mind – whether it is

to lie on a desk or be carried in the pocket,

to lie on a table or be held in the hand,

to be used often or seldom,

to be 'useful' or 'ornamental'.

A large subject will stand being written 'large', but it will also stand being written 'small'. A small subject, on the other hand, must seek a modest medium – written large it becomes immediately ridiculous. The student will find it stimulating to make books decidedly large or small: the necessities and opportunities of the case are then most apparent, and indeed go far to fulfil themselves. Thus it is more easy to make a great book grand or a little book pretty than it is to give interest of form to a medium-sized book.

It is proper to let the actual proportions of the leaf be finally decided by the shapes and sizes into which our ordinary skin of vellum or sheet of paper may be naturally cut or folded. We may, however, take such a skin or sheet as will give us something near our approximate choice. It is commonly known that the sizes of sheets of paper are traditional, and that a sheet folded once gives us a *folio*, folded again a *quarto*, and folded a third time an *octavo* – so that we know, for example, that the page of a 'Royal' quarto (or 'Roy. 4to') is one quarter (in area) of a 'Royal' sheet. But possibly it is not so well known that, in spite of the number and variety of the traditional sheets, the ratio of *length to breadth* in every case approximates to the ratio of $9:7$. And therefore, whatever the size, the proportions of the leaf of a book – that is, of its height to breadth – are approximately regular, being in the case of ('upright') folios and 8vos as $7:4\frac{1}{2}$, and in 4tos and 16mos as $9:7$ (30). It is a good plan to regard these as our regular proportions for leaves, only departing from them when we have a special reason and opportunity for so doing.

Generally the next thing to be settled (approximately) is the size (propor-

30. Showing the approximate proportions of traditional sheets and their foldings.

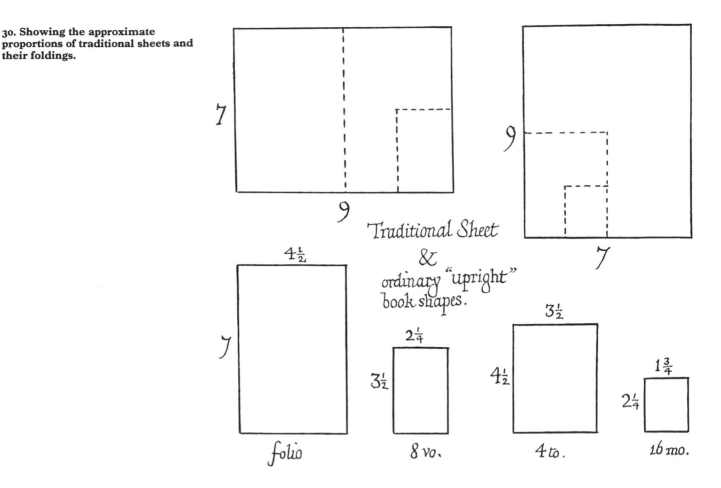

Traditional Sheet & ordinary "upright" book shapes.

folio   8 vo.   4 to.   16 mo.

tions) of the margins. In ordinary printed books the total area given to margins is about half the area of the page – that is, an equal area to that of the text column. The margins are generally greater or less than this accordingly as the books are better class or cheaper productions; though very small books (e.g. prayer books), even when fairly well produced, commonly have smaller margins for the sake of economy. All things considered there is no one thing that is greatly at fault in ordinary books, but the modern printer (or publisher) is too apt to be lavish of 'wide' margins without rhyme or reason in fancy publications, while he is almost criminally economical of them in cheap editions. The general subject of margins will be discussed further in another chapter: here we will consider them in certain special relations to books. The purpose of the margins is chiefly to make the text more readable by isolating or framing it: they are therefore essential to the normal book which is held in the hand and comparatively near the eye. Other books (such as desk books) where they are not so necessary still follow the fashion of the normal book.

In the case of a manuscript book we cannot do better than follow the ancient fashion as our ordinary rule. The margins of the medieval MSS commonly comprised more than half (say, three-fifths or more) of the page area. The ratio of their widths was about $1\frac{1}{2}:2:3:4$ (see figure 31, in which the names of the margins are shown on one page and their ratios on the other, and see also figure 29).

This fashion was the outcome of natural growth and use, and was the custom

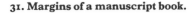

31. Margins of a manuscript book.

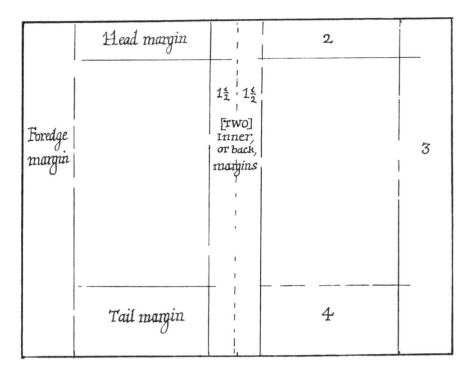

among people who valued books in a way that we can scarcely realize. We may therefore feel sure that it was not a case of 'art-nonsense' – as 'wide margins' and most of the trappings of the so-called 'decorative book-work' of the present day are apt to be.

We may attempt to explain the medieval margins thus. The previous statement that margins are essential to a book will be generally admitted, and it will be seen that as the reader's eye is focused on the page and is running forward and back along the lines of text, it adds greatly to his comfort if a wide fore-edge margin intercepts his eye from falling ('over the edge' as it were) upon the floor or walls or upon any other object of varied texture *on a near but different plane*.[1] The notably wide fore-edge margin of the medieval book does therefore add greatly to the reader's comfort and pleasure, in short, to the readableness of the book. It was the custom to make the two inner margins *together* approximately equal to the fore-edge margin. This breadth, although not so necessary as in the fore-edge margins, allowed for the loss of width that is apt to occur through the bending of the leaves at the middle fold. If we consider the two narrow inner margins – as they always come together – as forming one broad one (thus, $1\frac{1}{2}+1\frac{1}{2}=3$), it will be seen that the head margin is in effect the narrowest in the book, and we may reasonably suppose that the eye, running horizontally and having once read the headline, required no further margin there. The deep tail margin – sometimes very deep – was evidently allowed for a hand-hold and to prevent thumbing of the text. Its most important aspect that of *the space which is left* (after the page has been written) will be dealt with in the general discussion of margins.

Should anyone have difficulty in setting out margins, I offer the following formula for the common *folio* or *octavo* proportion of leaf, namely, $7:4\frac{1}{2}$ (30):

Make $\begin{cases} \text{Height of text column} = \text{width of page} \\ \text{Width of text column} = \text{two-fifths height of page.} \end{cases}$

[1] E.g. – a modern instance – his opposite neighbour in the 'Tube' – Publishers might do worse than try to read their own cheap editions in the 'Tube', with a view to discovering the limit.

The area of text will then = two-fifths area of page and this will allow the right proportions exactly $1\frac{1}{2}:2:3:4\frac{1}{5}$.[1]

Having, then, a given page and margins, we are left with a given space to fill with text; we have therefore to settle the treatment of *the line of writing*. The length of this line is already determined, so that our main concern is with the size of the letter. If there is no special consideration in favour of a special size of letter, we take that size of letter which will give us a convenient number of words to the line. The ordinary book has, speaking roughly, from eight to ten words in the line: to have much more than this, or to have much less, is very tiresome for the reader (27, III). The student who at first will not be able to 'pack' his words tightly may try about six words to the line. The average English word, with its succeeding space, takes about five letter-spaces; for a six-word line about thirty-two letter-spaces will be required. If, then, for example, our given writing-line be 8 inches long, this would allow of thirty-two letter-spaces of $\frac{1}{4}$ inch each. Roughly we may reckon the normal letter-space as a *square*, therefore in normal letters our 8-inch, six-word line will take $\frac{1}{4}$-inch writing.

We have still to settle the distance between the lines. It is best to allow too much space here rather than too little, but the normal course to follow is to allow the *ascenders* and *descenders* just to clear each other. Thus, if we put a p over a d, this will give us our line space, which, if fully spaced, will be about three times the height of the letter o (32). In the case of normal $\frac{1}{4}$-inch letters fully spaced, this will be $\frac{3}{4}$ inch. Our line-space thus given, we find how often it will go into the height of the given text space, and thus we get the number of lines to the page. Slight compromises are made in fitting all together, as, for example, if there is a little space over we may throw it into the tail margin.

Thus we may see in the matter of the size and shape of the book, of its margins, and of its writing and spacing how the work itself develops methods and how the broad outlines of the plan are, in a sense, settled for us. To *permit* this phenomenon is one of the first steps – and perhaps it is the last – in the 'practice' of design. Doubtless, to some, these things may all seem obvious, and there would indeed be no use in recapitulating them were it not for the gross or perverse misapprehension of elementary methods that is a feature of this advanced age. (The present writer does not claim to be entirely exempt.)

32. Example of normal letters fully spaced.

[1] From Pl. I. *Manuscript and Inscription Letters*, by the Author.
Corrigendum: I find that the formula given above actually gives margins of the ratio $1\frac{1}{2}:2:3:$ about $4\frac{1}{2}$ – allowing a rather deep tail margin.

Formal Penmanship

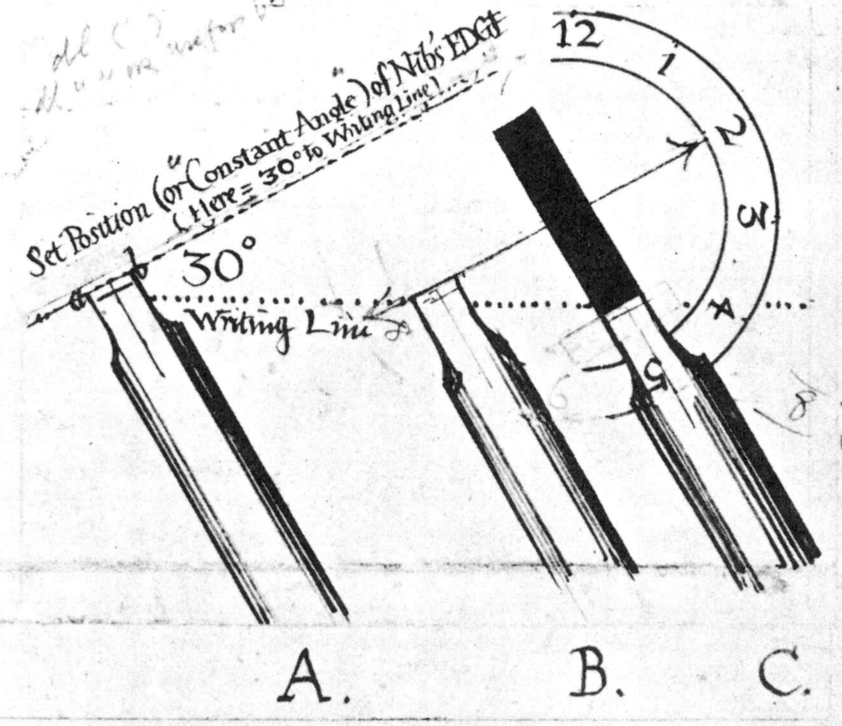

Fig. 1. Example of a (Bamboo) Formal Pen with a (¼ in.) Square-cut & Broad Nib ~~that has a~~ Sharp Edge (a —— b) ~~and Two Sharp Corners (a & b).~~

(A) The Nib is ^here^ shown held in a particular Set Position for Writing — viz., with its Edge at a Constant Angle of 30° to the Writing-Line.

(B) Held in that particular Set-Position it will make its ~~forward~~ Thinnest Stroke in the Direction of 2 o'clock (or 8 o'clock), ^(or onward and forward)^ and —

(C) it will make its Broadest Stroke in the Direction of 5 o'clock.

Note. The Set Position of 30° is given here as a good normal example of a "Constant Angle" (It is used for the MS. of the "Foundational Hand", p.). The Pen may be held in many other different Set Positions (from 0° to 90° in fact — i.e. between Edge Horizontal and Edge Vertical) for different Manuscripts.

In figure: 12 1 2 3 4 5 6 7 8 9

Set Position (or Constant Angle) of Nib's Edge (Here = 30° to Writing Line)

30°

Writing Line

A.   B.   C.

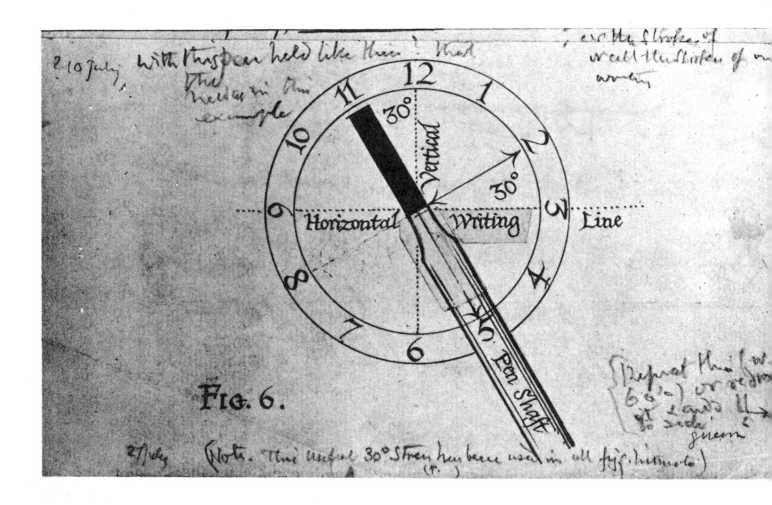

FIG. 6.

MS. re WEIGHT (of the Stroke Shapes) 27

Firstly, the WEIGHT may be varied. By using Wider or Narrower Nibs, we get Heavier or Lighter Stroke-Shapes. For example, the Strokes of figure 4, if we take a 5/16 in. Nib, we get the Heavyish Stroke-Shapes shown in figure 5.

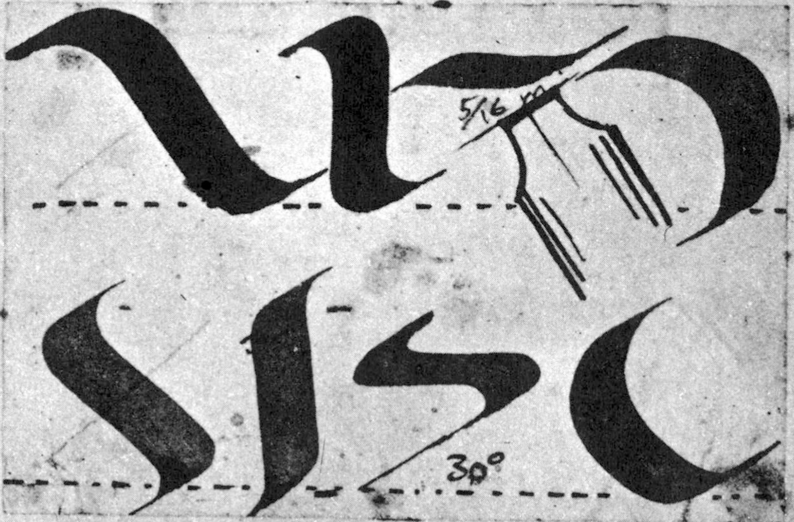

5/16 in.

30°

Fig. 5. The Strokes of Fig. 4 written with a 5/16 in. Nib become Heavyish Stroke-Shapes.

Again, if we write these Strokes with a 5/32 in. Nib, we get the Lightish Stroke-Shapes shown in figure 6.

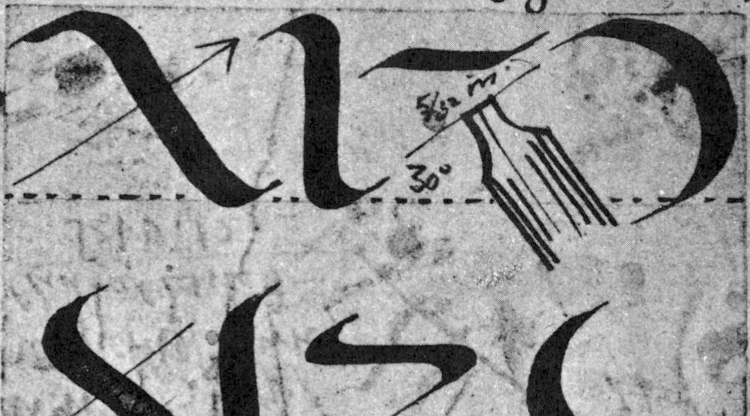

5/32 in.

30°

30°

Fig. 6. The Strokes of fig. 2 written with

By comparing figures 7 and 9 we may see how either Constant Angle gives its own characteristic _Shaping and Stressing_ to every Stroke. And it is clear that any two Formal Manuscripts which differ from each other in their Constant Angles must differ from each other in every Letter (see fig. 10).

roman
"Slanted Pen Writing" (Constant Angle abt. 35°)

roman
"Straight Pen Writing" (Const. Angle abt. Horizontal)

FIG. 10.

Note (1): The normal Thin Stroke, produced by moving the Nib edgeways, always coincides with the Constant Angle of any MS.. In practice therefore it is convenient to regard the Constant Angle as _the Angle of the Thin Stroke to the Writing Line_. The Thin Stroke forms a visible and simple clue to the Angle, whether we are examining an old MS. or deciding the precise position on the paper of the Edge of our own Nib.

Note (2): The two Constant Angles contrasted in figure 10, like those contrasted in the previous figures, broadly represent two important modes of Formal Writing, viz., Writing which has its _Thin Strokes Diagonal_ (as in writing with a "Slanted Pen"), and Writing which has its _Thin Strokes Approximately Horizontal_ (as in writing with a "Straight Pen"). These two modes I have, for many years, distinguished by the rather clumsy but descriptive terms of "_Slanted-Pen Writing_" and "_Straight-Pen Writing_".

Forenote on the meaning of Formal Penmanship

In any handicraft we can distinguish three main features, which may be called its 'Tools', its 'Traditions', and its 'Things'. TOOLS, including our hands and all other instruments and substances used, are its working-material basis. TRADITIONS, including all methods and models used, and the manners of our life and time, are its usages. THINGS, including the actual article to be made, and what we intend in making it, and what we do make of it, are its objectives. All three features join in embodying, animating, and inspiring the Craftsman's Creations.

Looking into one of these creations – some typical craftsman-made Thing – we are aware of its threefold nature. Its material, methodic, and imaginal properties – though physically, vitally, and inspirationally inseparable – are mentally distinguishable. And, by distinguishing these properties, and describing them, we can arrive at a general definition or description of a craft and form an elementary conception of its meaning.

The meaning of Formal Penmanship is described in this manner in the following three Parts of this book, which treat of its Tools, its Traditions, and its Things. This distinction of three features in a craft, and their overlapping and merging in the Thing, is dealt with further in Part III.

Note dated 16 July 1944

[In this note E.J. wrote as follows]: Thinking of the original order: Inspiring, Animating, Embodying, and alteration of a year ago to Embodying, Animating, Inspiring, to keep closer to the preparatory idea, thus the altered E, A, I order is best. My original thought had been especially that some THING (a piece of wood, ivory or vellum for example) may inspire the craftsman with the idea or ideal image – and also to cross the two statements thus 1, 2, 3, and 3, 2, 1 and to emphasize the idea that each is joined in each though specializing in itself.

I incline on reflection to the new order namely, embodying, animating and inspiring (partly to support the prefatory order and working-material-basis and partly because it is the logical order in the craftsman's creations, i.e. his works.)

But as I wish to overlap associated ideas, e.g. the Craftsman Creating and the Craftsman's Creations, it might be best to have both orders, or else after embodying, animating and inspiring the Craftsman's Creations (possibly in another paragraph) some statement that they 'Inspire the Craftsman, embody his idea and give it material life'.

But in a book for craftsmen the primary order is Genesis II, 7. 'And the Lord God formed man out of the dust of the ground, and breathed into his nostrils the breath of life; and man became a living soul.' Genesis II, 19 is also worth considering in this connexion:
'And out of the ground the Lord God
  formed every beast of the field,
  and every fowl of the air;
  and brought them unto Adam to see what he would
  call them;
  and whatsoever Adam called every living creature,
  that was the name thereof.'

Part I   Formal penmanship described by its tools

Chapter 1   The formal pen and its stroke shapes

The essential shape or features of the formal pen

Formal penmanship in its general sense implies any careful writing with a pen, but in the special sense used in this book it means formal writing with a broad nib that has a sharp edge and two sharp corners.

The pen may be made of any suitable material – quill, or bamboo, or steel – which will give a truly shaped and sufficiently durable nib. The typical nib is centrally split and must be stiffly springy. The 'cut' of the nib may differ for

1. Square-nibbed, and right and left oblique-nibbed varieties of the formal pen – each having a broad sharp edge (a to b) and two sharp corners (a and b). Large, cut bamboos.

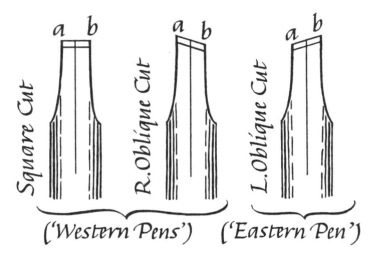

Square Cut   R. Oblique Cut   L. Oblique Cut

('Western Pens')   ('Eastern Pen')

different writings or for different penmen. Broadly speaking there are three main varieties of the essential shape of the formal pen, for the nib may be cut either Square, or Right Oblique, or Left Oblique, provided that we preserve the essential feature: a broad nib, sharp edged and sharp cornered.

Such a nib in normal use will make its own thick and thin strokes naturally (without pressing) in accordance with the set positions in which it is held and the different directions through which it is moved. Its thickest strokes have the breadth of the nib, and its thinnest the thinness of its edge.

The whole value and force and worth-doing-ness of formal penmanship comes from the fact that it is the product of this special tool, the formal pen as above defined. I have ventured to distinguish these differently cut pens of figure 1, as 'Western' and 'Eastern' pens, because square-cut and right-oblique nibs seem to me to have been chiefly used in the development of Western writing, and left-oblique nibs to have been used – perhaps exclusively – in the

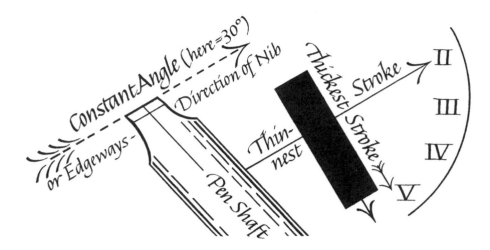

2. Example of a broad nib that has a sharp edge and two sharp corners and of the 'thin' and 'thick' strokes which this nib would produce if, held with its edge here shown pointing at 2 and 5 o'clock, or 'constant angle', it be moved through the directions of these strokes.

development of Eastern writing. The term 'formal pen' in this book will commonly mean a Western pen, with a broad nib that is either square-cut or that has some degree of right-obliquity. Note: In oblique cut nibs the amount or degree of obliquity may differ for different uses, but it must be limited; reasonably about 20° is probably a safe limit.

The corners of an oblique cut nib are, of course, one acute angle and one obtuse. The obtuse angle can still be sharp cornered by being cleanly cut and truly angular. Note: It is best that the scribe himself should as far as possible make or fashion his own pens to suit his particular requirements. Different materials have their own special advantages, especially in relation to the making of nibs of different widths for writing large or small. It is within reason and possibility that the modern penman might use formal nibs as narrow as $1/50$ inch, or less, or as broad as 1 inch, or more.

Large bamboo pens, cut about 8 or 9 inches long, with nibs from $\frac{3}{16}$ inch to $\frac{3}{8}$ inch broad, are very valuable to the student for study and experiments in formal writing (and he is advised here to provide himself with one as soon as possible). Very broad nibs such as these may have to be fitted with devices such as 'springs' or 'ink-wells' for holding the large quantity of ink that they require.

For modern scribes formal penmanship is, in fact, the characteristic product of a special tool – a nib's edge or a broad sharpened nib – a tool which we control, but which, at the same time, dominates what we make with it (as the potter's wheel might be said to dominate the work of the potter). Any skeleton or abstract form, on being written with our special pen, is automatically given the character of formal penmanship (as any lump of clay on the potter's wheel becomes roundly symmetrical, or pot-like).

The most notable and perhaps the most important virtue of the formal pen is this, that it has been the historic letter-making instrument, having practically created the innumerable types of lower-case from their stylus-made skeleton 'scribbled' form of the first to the third century.

The likeness between penmanship and printing is actually a family likeness, the early printing types having been copied directly from pen forms nearly 500 years ago. Instead of likening our pen-made letters to print, it would be

3. Skeleton forms and skeleton letters become 'Formal Penmanship' when rewritten with a broad-nibbed pen.

historically more correct to say that modern printing types retain a remarkable likeness to pen-made letters. The working virtue of our broad nib is that, by its own shape and by its natural movements in use, which are formal, uniform and swift, it gives a high degree of 'form' and 'uniformity' and 'controlled freedom', that is, a high degree of tool-character, to the letters made with it.

This formal-pen character in our manuscripts is most marked in the formality and regularity of the strokes, in the contrast of the thin and thick strokes, and the harmony of their incidence and the emphasis of their bias or 'stress', and in the easy flow of their recurrent ribbon-like shapes.

These clean-cut, harmoniously contrasting, and easy-flowing pen strokes

4. Example of a (bamboo) formal pen with a square-cut ¼-inch nib, held in a given set-position for writing, and examples of its thinnest stroke and its broadest stroke made when the nib is kept in that set-position.
A. The particular set-position in which the nib is held in this example is such that the edge makes a 'constant-angle' of 30° with the writing line.
B. Held in that particular set-position it will make its thinnest stroke either forward towards the direction of 2 o'clock or backward towards 8 o'clock.
C. And it will make its broadest stroke (down-and-forward only) in the direction of 5 o'clock.

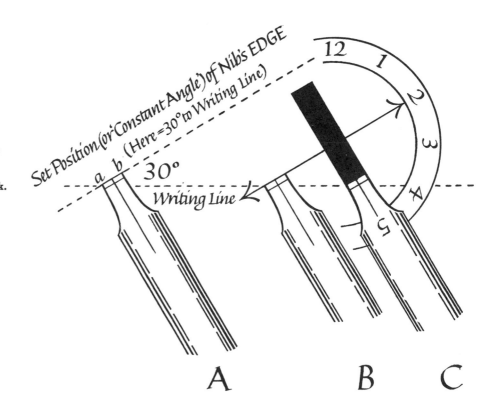

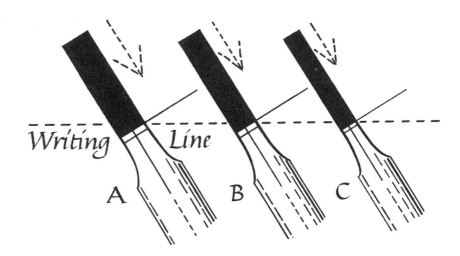

5. Three different breadth-strokes produced by three different nib widths (in three different scripts). At A. the stroke and the nib are each ⅛ inch wide; at B. they are ¼ inch wide; at C. they are ⅜ inch wide.

The arrows indicate the direction in which the three strokes are made, that is, the direction in which the three nibs were moved. Note: Each pen-shaft is here shown held at the same easy slant (or set-position).

Note: Strokes having intermediate widths are made by the nib moving in directions between edgeways and breadthways.

spring from the sharp edge of the broad nib, from the differences between the weight of the width-stroke and the lightness of its edge-stroke, and from its naturally swift and uniform movements, making easy and uniform repetition of similar parts or strokes and giving to each part a shape and a degree of weight in absolute relation to the position or direction of the part and to the direction of the edge of the nib. Note: The set-position of 30° is given here as a normal and useful example of a constant angle, and an important instance of its use is the writing of the foundational hand. The pen may be held in many different set-positions, for different kinds of formal writings, say, from about 0° to 90°, that is from 'edge' horizontal to 'edge' vertical.

An example of 45° is given in figure 7. The same pen held so that its constant angle is 45° makes its thinnest strokes towards 1.30 o'clock or towards 7.30 o'clock and its broadest strokes towards 4.30 o'clock. In formal penmanship a special importance is attached to the thinnest strokes which we call hair-strokes and to the thickest, or broadest strokes which we will call broad strokes.

The thinnest stroke is made by the nib moving edgeways; it is always a hair-line and as thin as the nib's edge is sharp.

The broadest stroke is made by the nib moving breadthways; its width is the width of the nib which writes it.

The modern scribe decides the width of the broadest stroke by choosing the width of the nib with which he will write a manuscript;[1] commonly he himself cuts the nib of the pen to a special shape and measure.

He also decides the positions (or clock directions, see figure 6) of the thinnest and the broadest strokes by the set-position in which he holds the nib's edge while writing a given manuscript.

Note: The position or lie of the thinnest, or hair, stroke is always the same as the position or lie of the nib's edge on the paper; the position of the broadest stroke is always at right angles to that of the thinnest stroke. (For example as in figure 4,c.)

It is clear then, that in the writing of any given manuscript, the actual width of the nib used by the scribe (especially in relation to the size or height

[1] In his original text E.J. uses the word *manuscript* (almost invariably abbreviated to MS) to mean written by hand, not printed. He also uses *manuscript* to mean a book written by hand or a MS book. *Ed.*

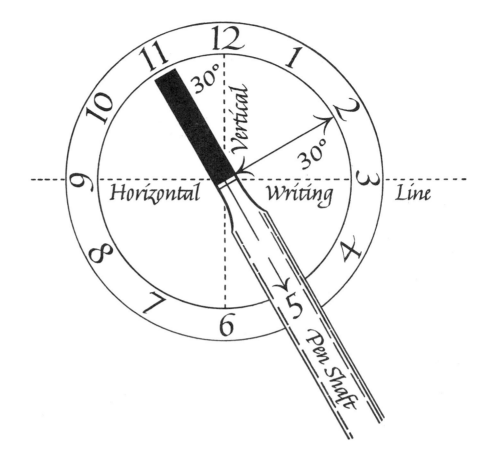

6. The clock directions of the thinnest and the broadest strokes.
Note: This useful 30° stress has been used in all figures hitherto.

of the writing) and also the actual set-position of the nib's edge on the paper (due to its 'cut', and to the 'slant' at which he holds the pen) are very important. Indeed these two writing conditions (which include the traditional nib-cuts of the past) have been for centuries, and still are, the chief tool-factors in the characterization of the letter-forms and the writing of formal manuscripts.

How the penman starts

A penman before beginning any manuscript necessarily either adopts or chooses the writing conditions for it. As regards dimensions, he has to fix or set three particular measurements for the writing of each particular manuscript. First, probably, he will set the letter-height, that is the size of the writing; then the nib-width; then the degree of the constant angle, that is the angle formed on the paper by the set-position of the nib's edge to the writing line. Here we may note that in any given formal manuscript the constant angle is most easily seen and measured as the particular angle the hair-stroke of the writing makes with the ruled writing-lines. And it may be truly said of our formal penmanship that, whenever he writes, the penman fixes the pen or writing conditions for a particular manuscript, and so dominant is the pen, that the chosen conditions will then mark and characterize every stroke of that particular manuscript.

7. Examples of a square-nibbed pen held in two different set-positions (A and B), giving respectively constant angles of 30° and 45° (for use in different manuscripts).

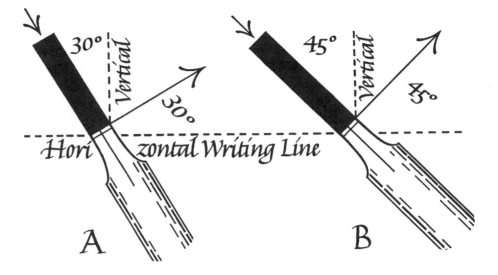

8. A square-nibbed pen held in four different positions, and the corresponding positions or lies of its breadth stroke. This pen's nib being square-cut, its pen-shaft and the breadth strokes have similar 'slants' or inclinations from the vertical. Expressed in degrees the inclinations are respectively 0°, 30°, 45°, and 90°, and the stresses which they would give to four different manuscripts may be called upright, slanted 30° and 45°, and horizontal.

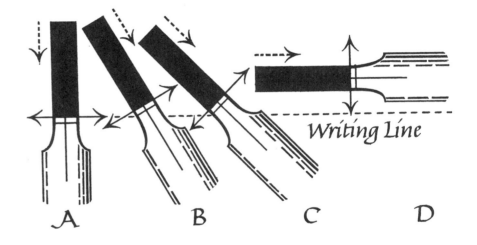

9. Seven breadth-stroke positions typifying the range of practicable manuscript stresses from upright to horizontal. The seven arrows represent the downward and forward directions in which the pen was moved when making the breadth-strokes.

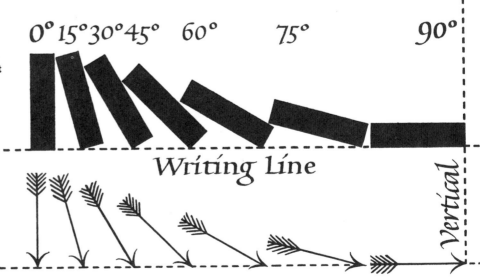

Variation of manuscript stress:
To produce varieties of Formal Penmanship by the proper position or orientation of thicks and thins

The specific stress of any given formal manuscript may be identified with, and measured by, the regular fall or lie of its heaviest breadth stroke.

For example (7), the breadth stroke shown at A falls with an inclination from the vertical of 30°. And, if we wrote with a pen like that (at A) held like that (at A) our writing would have a tilted 30° stress.

But if we wrote another manuscript with the same pen held as at B, which makes the breadth stroke incline 45°, that manuscript would have a tilted 45° stress.

The two examples in figure 7 show that holding the same pen at a different slant produces a different stress. And it follows that to keep any given writing uniform we must keep the slant of the pen uniform.

We will now go briefly into the technique of producing specific stresses, firstly observing how the nature and extent of stress variation depend on the natural action of the hand-and-pen in writing. Thus, when we write the normal strokes of formal penmanship, we hold the pen naturally, that is with as comfortable a slant to the right as we may; but we move the pen naturally, that is to say, we commonly, in breadth stroke movements, almost always draw the pen towards us and/or towards the right.

Controlled by that natural action of hand-and-pen, the various positions in which our breadth strokes can be made to fall range approximately from the downward vertical to the forward horizontal. That is to say practicable manuscript stresses may range from about UPRIGHT stress – through unlimited TILTED stresses – to about HORIZONTAL stress. This range is typified in figure 8.

From figure 8 we can deduce two helpful general ideas; first, square-nibs, that is pens having their nibs square-cut as in figure 8, will always make their breadth strokes fall in line with the pen-shaft; therefore, the degree of slant at which we hold a square-nibbed pen, for any manuscript, will be the degree of stress of that manuscript (30°, 45°, etc.). Second, the hair-stroke of the formal pen (whatever the cut of its nib) is always at right angles to the breadth stroke; therefore, if the breadth stroke has a tilt (from the vertical) the hair stroke has a similar tilt (from the horizontal).

On page 74 it was said that the modern scribe determines the lie or clock positions of both strokes, the thinnest and the broadest, by the set-position in which he holds the nib's edge while writing. That tells in brief how we give a specific stress to any formal manuscript.

We see in figure 8 that, because the nib is square-cut, the pen's shaft is exactly in line with the breadth-stroke and has the same inclination or slant of 30°. It is clear that simply by holding this pen at different slants we could make the breadth stroke fall in correspondingly different directions, and so change its stress, through a range of at least 90°, from vertical to horizontal. Now it would be possible, with a square-cut nib, to write any one of the breadth strokes in figure 9 by holding the pen at the same slant as the stroke (for example as the two strokes in figure 7 were written), but only for strokes near the centre of the range should we find it really easy, because only near the centre of the range would the pen slants be really comfortable to hold.

I suggest that for the average person's hand, the really comfortable pen slants are from about 45° to 60°. And, though different person's hands vary, it would be generally agreed that to hold the pen much straighter than 45° or more slanted than 60° would be less comfortable.

In practice, however, the modern penman (who writes a number of different manuscript hands) gets the exact stress required in any one manuscript partly by holding the pen at a suitable and convenient slant, and partly by cutting the nib for the writing with a supplementary edge-slant which permits easier

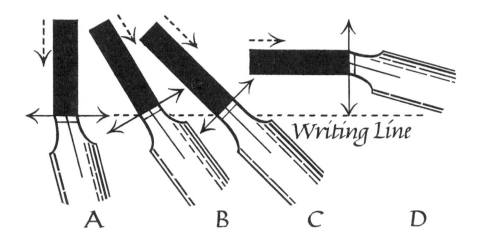

10. Four different pens each specially cut (and specially held). A and B have edge-slants to the right; C is square-cut; D has an edge-slant to the left.

handling. The arrow shows the direction through which the pen has been moved – while keeping its set (pen) slant unchanged – in making the strokes. The relation of the edge of the nib to the paths of the strokes is as follows:

The EDGE of the nib is at right angles to the 11 o'clock path
somewhat oblique to the 12 o'clock path
very oblique to the 1 o'clock path
coincident with the 2 o'clock path
very oblique to the 3 o'clock path

The scribe cuts his nibs with various edges to the right (10,A) for stresses which approximate to the upright. Even for the slanted 30° some, I for one, cut the nib's edge a little to the right (10,B).

The pen-shaft slanted at 45° lies so naturally in the hand, and is so easily held, that for that stress I think most scribes would cut the nib square (10,C).

For stresses which approximate to the horizontal (uncommon in the West, but proper for Hebrew and other Eastern writings) we would cut the edge-slants to the left (10,D).

All such adjustments of cutting and holding the pen vary according to the individual scribe who, in writing any given manuscript, tries to get as easy a hold for his own hand as he can, without over cutting the edge-slant, for which the limit is about 20°.

Let the reader note well that though such adjustment of special cutting and special holding aims at ease and freedom for the scribe's hand, its primary object is to secure the exact given set-position of the nib's edge in relation to the writing-line which will give the required stresss.

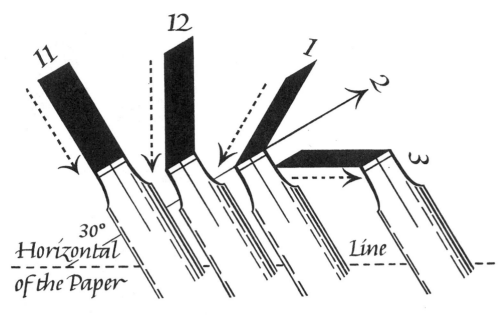

11. The same pen, held at the same slant, making the five strokes (in the 11, 12, 1, 2, and 3 o'clock positions) and showing the conditioning of set-widths by the edge set at 30° to the horizontal.

With the nib's edge at 45°
Verticals and horizontals
R. oblique (L. oblique = thinnest)
R. and L. oblique curves
Note the dexterwise bias

With the nib's edge horizontal
Verticals (horizontals = thinnest)
R. and L. obliques
R. and L. upright curves
Note the vertical bias

12. Some elementary stroke-shapes in medium length, short and very short, plain pen strokes, made with the same pen at two different constant angles, a. 45° and b. horizontal. The curves are best described as Decrescent and Increscent.

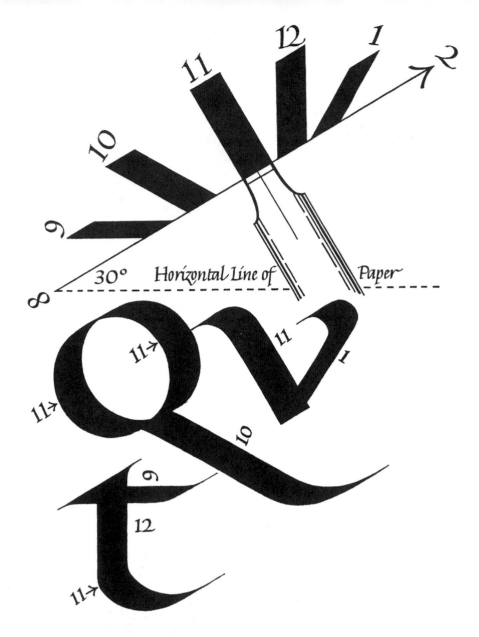

The nib's edge, by its particular position (or constant angle), gives a particular bias (or 'stress') to the writing, allotting to each different stroke a degree of width (or 'weight') in accordance with the relative positions of the stroke and the nib.

The nib's edge, by its actual width, gives actual 'weight' to the strokes (according to the bias – as above). It also gives apparent 'weight' to the letters according to the relative sizes of the nib and the writing as in figure 18.

Finally, the nib's edge (by its constant angle and width, together) gives, to each particular stroke, a particular shape geometrically in accordance with the position and size relations existing between the nib and the stroke. Thus the nature of the pen stroke shape is directional and dimensional.

How the reader may start

Let us now study the action of the formal pen in making various, simple strokes – diagonals, verticals, horizontals, and curves. For this purpose we will adopt the three measurements or writing conditions already used in figure 4; that is, we will take, or make, a bamboo pen, cut square like that in figure 4, with a nib *a quarter of an inch wide*; we will write with it our various strokes *standing about one inch high* – and, while writing these strokes, we will hold the pen slanted exactly as in figure 14, so that the edge of the nib touches the 'paper' *at an angle of thirty degrees with the writing-lines* all the time.

It may be noted that (for reasons explained later) we will start all these strokes (except the plain hair-strokes themselves) with a short hair-line and a curve, and finish with a short curve and a hairline.

Now we begin:

The ¼ inch nib's sharp edge, held and kept in its 30° set-position on the 'paper', and moved by the scribe's hand, without any appreciable pressure, lays down the inked strokes – determining their widths exactly according to its own direction of movement at any given moment. And its two sharp, truly angular corners sharply define the two sides or edges of each stroke, so that all the strokes (save the thin hair strokes) are clear cut, geometrically perfect shapes – as in most of our modern work – of the nature of parallelograms terminated by 'crescentic' parts, and of 'crescents'.

Sharpness is the first essential virtue in formal penmanship, and the true formal pen – given suitable ink and suitable 'paper' (and fair handling) – naturally and automatically produces for us these sharply edged, geometric, ribbon-like silhouettes or stroke-shapes which form the *elements of our letters* and are in themselves the chief characteristic of our work (14).

How the pen strokes may be varied

By changing the nib's width and/or the set-position of its edge on the 'paper' the formal pen will produce such simple, natural stroke-shapes or letter-strokes, in infinite variety of character.

14. Some typical stroke-shapes produced by simple movements of a formal pen made from a slender bamboo with a square-cut nib ¼ inch wide. The arrows show the directions in which the nib was moved. The two long arrows indicate the *forward* and the *backward* plain hair-strokes. The nib of the pen shows the set-position (or the 'slant') in which the pen was held (and kept unchanged) throughout the writing of all these strokes. Note the different pen movements; the upper four strokes are begun with a forward hair-line and the second four strokes are begun with a backward hair-line.

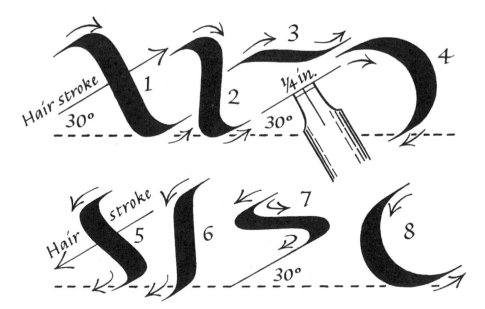

Changing the width of the nib – in relation to the stroke-length or letter-height – changes the relative WEIGHT of the stroke-shapes, and so gives us writings which are comparatively heavy, medium, or light.

Changing the set-position of the nib's edge changes the specific stress or lie of the stroke-shapes, and so gives us writings which differ from each other in the proper positions (or orientation) of their thicks and thins.

But besides giving (relative) weight and (specific) stress to all its letter-strokes the pen must be moved and directed by the scribe that it gives each stroke a third feature, a (particular) plan or LETTER-FORM. That is to say, the pen must be so handled by the scribe, in forming the different strokes, and in joining them together to make letters, that each stroke has *the right shape for a given part of a letter in a given form of alphabet*. A (particular) letter-form also implies that there is a *family likeness* among the different letters of any given alphabet which necessitates a family likeness among all its different stroke-shapes.

In practice the penman is chiefly concerned with the conventional forms of the strokes used in writing such alphabets as

small roman black-letter *italic*

which typify the accepted forms of 'small-letters' (or *printer's* 'lower-case') open to our choice. And as these three alphabets were first fashioned by the formal pen in the hands of the ancient scribes, we find our pen particularly apt in helping us to write similar or like alphabets by copying or imitating the forms of the original letter-strokes. In fact many of the manuscript originals of these letters were simple and direct penwork which can be almost automatically recreated by the same pen in the hand of the modern penman, and – better still – may be recreated with proper, small variations in the genesis of which the pen seems to prompt the writer.

The pen and the three writing factors

The remarkable formativeness of the formal pen, its special aptitudes for making and writing letters, and the traditions of its use have given it an historic and authoritative position as *the* letter-making tool, which makes it the very basis of our work. These properties of the tool will be dealt with later, but let it be noted here that they are bound up with the three features natural to its stroke-shapes, namely, weight, stress, and letter-form – which are now to be discussed. Note, moreover, that weight, stress, and letter-form are the three primary writing factors – by the varying of which, different varieties of formal writing have been produced by the scribes of the past, and, (if we are keen enough) may yet be produced by us.

Chapter 2 Varieties of writing produced by pen weight or writing heavier, and writing lighter

The relative weight of the stroke-shapes is kept constant in any one piece of writing, but it can be varied for different manuscripts. By using wider or narrower nibs for the same letter-height we get heavier or lighter stroke-shapes.

For example, the strokes in figure 14, which stand 1 inch high and were written with a ¼-inch nib may be taken to represent medium writing weight. If we now take a ⁵⁄₁₆-inch nib and rewrite them, we get the heavyish stroke-shapes shown in figure 15. Again, if we write the same strokes with a ³⁄₁₆-inch nib, we get the light stroke-shapes shown in figure 16.

In the above examples of stroke-shapes of various weights (14, 15, 16) – typifying what we may call medium, heavy, and light writing – we see that, although the fundamental, geometric nature of the stroke-shapes is unchanged, their actual shapes do change with their weights and show marked differences in their character.

Assuming that the medium weight stroke-shapes of figure 14 have approximately *normal widths*, we may note the more obvious of the differences in heavy and light stroke-shapes respectively – and contrast figures 15 and 16 – thus:

The chief features of heavy writing strokes

The heavy strokes in figure 15, having extra width (in the same length)
are   (1) noticeably plump
with (2) a dumpy trend
they (3) occupy more room and, as it were, encroach on their background
        space;
and (4) their curves have a more abrupt gradation (i.e. being fatter, the curves
        change more quickly in passing from thin to thick or from thick to
        thin).

The chief features of light writing strokes

The light strokes in figure 16, having less width (in the same length)
are   (1) noticeably slender,
with (2) an elongated trend;
they (3) take up less room and leave their backgrounds more open;
and (4) their curves have a more gradual gradation (i.e. being slenderer, the
        curves change more slowly in passing from thin to thick and from
        thick to thin).

15. The strokes of figure 14 written with a 5/16-inch nib become heavy stroke-shapes.

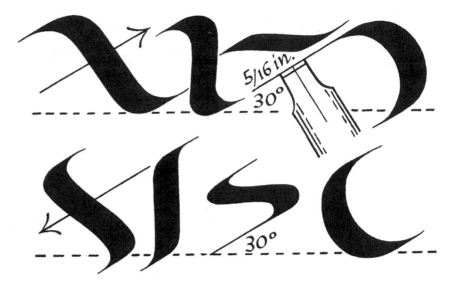

An effect of tone difference

An apparent tone difference (familiar to us all in the contrast made by a large, black chapter-initial in a page of ordinary print) may also be noted here, for its effects are important. Though they are equally black, yet heavy strokes *look blacker* in comparison, and light strokes *look greyer*. In both heavy and light manuscripts these effects are greatly enhanced by the background differences, and also by the cumulative force of letters in lines and pages, so that whole books are caused to look dark or light.

Effects of change of weight on pen-made letters

When stroke-shapes are joined together to make letters, the effects of their relative weights on the letter-forms are very marked. In any kind of lettering (as in all material things) any change of weight is a structural change. And in the case of formal penmanship, where the component letter strokes are 'geometrically perfect SHAPES' rhythmically 'passing from thin to thick and from thick to thin', changing the relative weight changes the letter-forms more or less obviously in every part. Different weights, therefore, produce different varieties of formal writing.

Copying and matching strokes for letters

We will now join some of our stroke-shapes together to form letters, and then make an experimental comparison of heavy and light writing. We begin by copying some of the medium weight strokes in figure 14 which come from a particular manuscript hand[1] and are written 1 inch high to show the shapes clearly; and after we have written a short word (*viz.*, 'ora') in this particular hand, we will write heavy and light varieties of it by using a broader pen and a narrower pen respectively.

[1] The Foundational Hand. *Ed.*

84

16. The strokes of figure 14 written with a $\frac{3}{16}$-inch nib become light stroke-shapes.

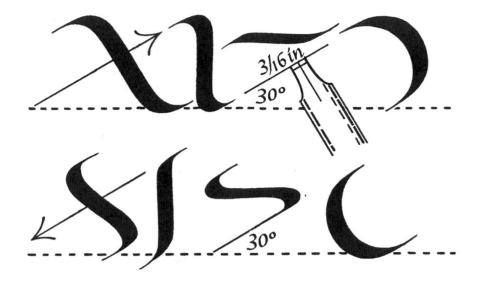

First with the same ($\frac{1}{4}$-inch) pen with which the medium weight strokes of figure 14 were written, and keeping the nib in the same (30°) set-position in which it was held during the writing of figure 14, we will copy successively the eighth, the fourth, and the second of the stroke-shapes in that figure, and also the plain, forward hair-stroke. These give us the two curves of o, the stem of r, and a bit of the loop of a (17,A).

To complete the letters we need an arm stroke for r, and a *stem-and-beak* stroke and a part loop for a. Taking the plans of these strokes from figure 16, i.e. the lighter example of the hand in figure 14, with our $\frac{1}{4}$-inch nib in the 30°

17A. Three stroke-shapes and a hair-stroke from figure 14.
B. Three new stroke-shapes made to match the above.
C. The seven strokes joined, forming the word 'ora'.
The writing shows a particular manuscript hand (large) as an example of a relatively medium weight script.

set-position, we follow (but lengthen) their tracks. We lengthen their tracks to suit our present 1-inch writing, but our ¼-inch nib broadens them in proportion and so preserves their relative weight and shapes. Thus the pen makes the three new shapes to match (17,B).[1]

Note: The student will see that using the same pen with which the original strokes were written (or a similar nib-width) and holding the pen at the same slant with which it was originally held (or with a similar set-position) are necessary conditions for making true copies. He will also find that they make both copying and matching largely automatic. That is to say, while he follows the correct tracks of the strokes, the set width and position of his nib automatically give to every stroke and to every part of every stroke its proper width and stress.

Joining stroke-shapes to make letters and words

Now we take the seven strokes (at figure 17,A,B) in their proper order, and, with the same pen held as before, we rewrite them, joining them together as we write them according to the nature of this hand – both stroke to stroke and – where it falls convenient – letter to letter. In this particular hand most of the strokes are begun and finished with short hair-lines (17,A,B). And here when one stroke is to be joined to another, the joining consists in *overlapping* a hair-line upon or with – and merging it in – the thicker stroke to which it is to be connected. The effect is that the joined hair-lines – though actually written by the pen – disappear, leaving points of contact only. The unjoined hair-lines are left as natural terminals (see the word 'ora' at figure 17,C).

The question of joining strokes depends on their nature and on the nature of the writing. But it may be noted here that the stroke-shapes of formal scripts, though written very swiftly, are generally set down each separately and complete – almost in a staccato manner – and that their joining appears to the eye rather as a matter of their contacts, their harmonious juxtaposition, and their even spacing.

Examples of medium weight and of heavy and light scripts

In the last figure the word 'ora' is written with a ¼-inch nib, and the height of its letters is 1 inch, or four times the width of the nib. That ratio, *viz., letter-height to nib-width = four to one*, represents, I think, approximately medium relative weight, in any normal, 'round', small-letter, formal script in which the stress tilts the o (such as the letters in figure 18) to which it applies.

We will now write this word with the broader $\frac{5}{16}$-inch pen, and, again with the ¼-inch pen, and then with the narrower $\frac{3}{16}$-inch pen. This gives us three brief examples representing heavy, medium and light writing, in which we find that the heavy and light scripts are varieties of the medium, and we will compare their characteristic differences (18,A). It is perhaps even more instructive to use the same pen and write different letter heights (18,B).

On the right of figure 18,A is illustrated a simple, accurate method for measuring the relative weights of formal scripts. The relative weight of any given formal script may be identified with and measured by the width of its

[1] The stem and beak stroke for a is based on the top of stroke 4 in figure 14, and of course combines the stem-stroke of 2 and the loop of stroke 8 in that figure. *Ed.*

18A. Examples of heavy, medium, and light writing showing some of the typical effects of different pen widths on letter-forms of the same height. The three varieties of manuscript which, though they are the same in their height, letter-shape and constant-angle, are made different by their weights, through being written with pens of different nib-widths.

18B. Examples of heavy, medium and light writing made by using the ¼-inch nib for letters three, four, and five nib-widths high.

broadest, or breadthways stroke. And, as that stroke has the same width as the nib with which it is written, we may measure the stroke length or letter height of any writing with the nib itself, or in old manuscripts, for example, with a nib specially cut to the same width. We can then describe the comparative weights of different scripts by their respective ratios of (so-many) nib-widths (or breadth strokes) of the letter height. This simple and accurate method, illustrated in figure 18,A, shows that the heavy, medium, and light manuscripts there – each measured by means of its own nib – are respectively three, four, and six nib-widths high.

Figure 18,A shows a striking example of the effects of weight on pen-made letter-forms, in the differences in the white inner backgrounds of the three o's. As we look from heavy to medium and then to light these white inside shapes change from the shape of a pointed leaf (in the heavy o), to a broad, almost oval shape (in the light o). We see in this the 'encroached-on' background of the heavy writing contrasted with the 'open' background of the light writing, and we note that these inside backgrounds – which outline the internal anatomy of the three o's – differ markedly in shape as well as in size.

Note: To make a habit of observing such inside shapes or 'counters' is very helpful to the student, for the counters of letters give us an important (yet often overlooked) clue to the real nature or structure of the letter-forms.

The differences we have just seen in the counters of these three o's and other differences – mentioned below – amount to structural differences in the letter-forms of the three scripts.

The medium script, as already noted, represents the normal weight and form of a particular hand. The heavy script and the light script – produced by writing this hand the same height, but with a broader pen and a narrower pen respectively – clearly belong to the same class or kind of writing as the medium script, but are distinct varieties of that script, differing from it in their letter-forms as well as in their weights.

The typical differences of these varieties may be indicated by summing up the distinctive features – the effects of greater weight – which we can see in the heavy o in figure 18,A, thus:

(1) The heavy o is more massive,
     its letter-form has a dumpy appearance,
(2) its equatorial diameter is greater,
     its axial diameter is less,
     its counter is narrower,
(3) its counter is more pointed,
(4) its curves have fatter-shaped 'crescents'.

Note: If the heavy alphabet were completed, all its letters would have the first three features of its o; and all the letters with curved counters (such as a b c d e f g h m n p q s t u – and perhaps others) would have both features of the o counter and also the fatter-shaped crescents (in part and modified according to the forms of their individual curves).

The distinctive features of the light o (etc.) are the typical reverse of the heavy o features. Comparatively the light o is clearly less massive, has an elongated appearance, less equatorial diameter, a wider counter, a less pointed counter, and slenderer-shaped crescents.

The r (etc.) and dumpiness and elongation

Very important effects – both in graphic forms and in appearances and in tendencies – are connected with the dumpy 'trend' of heavy penmanship and the elongated trend of light penmanship. Some of these effects may be seen in the heavy and light o's, but they are particularly well illustrated by the r's in figure 18,A. For example, in the heavy script the shape of the arm of the r is like a flowing lozenge, and, being about as broad as its own length, it has an appearance of shortness. In the light script the arm is like a wavy band, and, being nearly twice as long as its own breadth, it has an appearance of comparative length (18,A).

Again, in the heavy r the stem – between its head-hook and its foot-hook – is in fact a little shorter than the stem of the light r, but appears much shorter.

Indeed when one looks at the three writings in figure 18,A, though every letter there is the same height, it is difficult to resist the illusion that the heavy script is shorter and the light script taller. The truth behind the illusion is the fact that relatively to its pen-width the heavy script *is* shorter (i.e., its height is only about three times its pen-width), and that relatively to its pen-width the light script *is* taller (its height being about five times its pen-width).

For describing the weights of manuscripts, such as those in figure 18,A and kindred types, viz.: 'round' or 'uncompressed' small-letters – such as the reformed Caroline minuscule[1] or any manuscript forms resembling roman lower-case print – the following table is convenient and, I believe, optically sound:

'Round' MSS are				
Heavy	Height of the	*Three*	of their nib-widths
Medium	letter about	*Four*	or breadth strokes
Light	(or over)	*Five*	

Note: The letter height to be measured is the height of the bodies of the small letters – typified by o, r, a, in figure 18,A regardless of the height of ascenders and descenders, such as b, p, etc.

The above mode of stating the weight ratio gives the letter height as a multiple of the nib-width (or breadth stroke). We sometimes prefer to put the ratio the other way and express the comparative weight of a writing by giving the nib-width (or breadth stroke) as a fraction of the letter height.

In that case the formula becomes:

'Round' MSS are				
Heavy	if the width of	*One third*	of their
Medium	their breadth	*One fourth*	letter
Light	stroke is about	*One fifth* (*or less*)	height

Weight is of fundamental importance in all lettering. Its effects are peculiarly marked in formal penmanship, where the actual widths of all the different strokes are geometrically governed by the pen itself and vary regularly and rhythmically between the full breadth of the nib (however broad) and theoretically a thin hair-line. We have just seen three different varieties of manuscript produced by almost literally the same movements of a heavy pen, a medium pen, and a light pen. Besides such characteristic effects as we have just noted there are tendencies arising from the use of relatively broader and relatively narrower nibbed pens which may perhaps be very briefly and generally stated thus: it seems as though a medium pen promoted legibility, a heavy pen promoted Gothic character, and a light pen promoted Roman character.

[1] E.g. BM, Harley MS. 2904. *Ed.*

Chapter 3 The three primary factors or writing conditions

Three primary conditions determine the special character of any manuscript made with the formal pen. They are the WEIGHT of the stroke, the ANGLE which gives the 'stress', and the FORM of the letter.

We may take any formal manuscript for a model, and, by copying its special weight, angle and letter-form, make a very close copy of it; or, by modifying one or more of those special conditions, produce a variety of it.

Specific conditions of weight, angle, and lettter form – whether habitually followed or deliberately chosen – are, in effect, set by the penman each time that he begins a piece of writing, and they are kept constant by him until that piece of writing is finished.

The character of formal penmanship depends primarily upon these three set conditions – or relations of the nib's edge to the manuscript:

19A. The Weight of the manuscript.

(A) *The width of the nib's edge – or 'the weight' of the MS* in relation to the size of the writing (e.g., the nib's width may be *set* wide, or medium, or narrow, for the same size or height of lettter).

19B. The Angle of the manuscript.

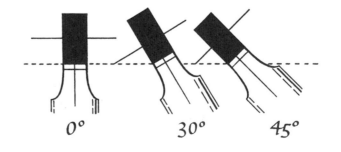

0°   30°   45°

(B) *The position of the nib's edge – or 'the angle' of the MS (or 'the constant angle')* in relation to the horizontal line of writing (e.g., the nib's edge may be *set* parallel with, or inclined to, or much inclined to the horizontal line).

19C. The Form of the manuscript.

30°   0°   45°

(C) *The positions (and lengths) of the strokes – or 'the form' of the MS (or the letter-form*) in relation to the position and width of the nib's edge (e.g., some parts (or strokes) of the letters will be parallel with, some perpendicular to, and some inclined to the nib's edge position. Also, especially in different alphabets, the lengths of kindred strokes vary).

These three conditions differ appropriately in different kinds of writing (e.g., in roman and italic, in 'heavy' writing and 'light' writing, and in other varieties). But, in any given piece of writing, they are normally kept constant. Their constancy, in fact, maintains the character which they create.

As the penman commonly uses certain forms and sizes of letters, so also, when writing, he automatically adopts the pen-slant and nib-width – that is to say, the angle and weight – that he is used to. But, by selecting special angles, weights, and letter-forms (or even modifying the normal forms), he can either copy unfamiliar hands or invent new varieties. Yet, if properly made, these varieties will turn out to be pen creations: their character will be dominated by the chosen angle and weight. In short, the penman sets the conditions, he is free to choose and impose his will on the manuscript, but, allowing for the parts played by paper, ink and other tools, the ultimate effects of his choice are predestined by the pen.

Because of their primary importance the three writing conditions are here briefly described.

The weight

The weight of the writing will be heavy, medium or light, according as the penman uses a broad, medium, or narrow nib for the particular manuscript he has in hand.

The weight may be described as the relation of the width of the pen's broadest stroke to the height of the letters. And, as the width of the broadest stroke is given by the breadth of the nib, this ratio is most conveniently expressed – and measured – in nib-widths as indicated in figure 20. This illustration shows sufficiently well, for the present purpose, the meaning of manuscript weight.

Weight is of fundamental importance in lettering. Its effects are peculiarly marked in formal penmanship, where the changes in weight produce a number of interesting results.

One such result may be noted here in passing. A change in weight in the

20. Heavy, medium and light writing, or writing of about three, four, and five nib-widths (high).

writing of any formal manuscript is necessarily accompanied by a change in the shapes of all the letters. Though they may appear to retain much of the same generic letter form, their actual letter form is altered. This is well illustrated by the *inside shapes* of the three O's in figure 20.

To the penman the most interesting effect of weight (and one bearing on the example just given) is that the heavier the writing the more it is dominated by the pen.

The constant angle

(I add the word 'constant', to mark its importance in this factor.) It may be described as the angle which the thinnest stroke makes to the writing line.

21. Nib's edge (a–b) set at an angle of 45° to the writing line (W.L.).

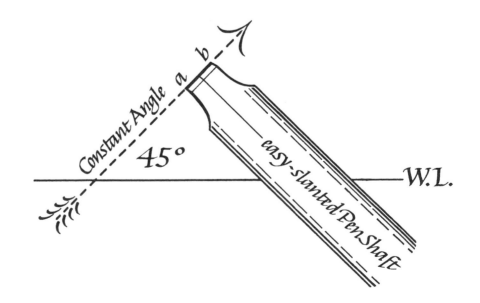

22. The six strokes as shaped by the nib's edge kept at an angle of 45°.

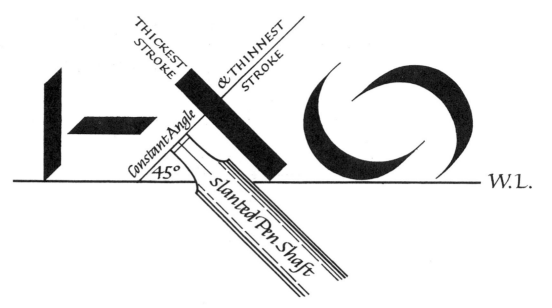

The constant angle of any writing denotes the set position of the nib's edge in that writing. That position sets the positions of the thick and thin strokes, and so gives the characteristic STRESS of that writing.

It may be described as the angle which the edge of the nib makes with the writing line. For example, if the pen shaft is held at an easy slant (as in figure 21), and if the nib is square-cut, we get a constant angle of about 45°.

If, with the nib's edge in this position (i.e. constantly at the angle of 45° to the writing line), we write these six strokes – the vertical, the horizontal, the two diagonals, and the two full curves – we get the stroke shapes shown in figure 22.

In these slanted-pen stroke-shapes note especially the following points:
The thinnest stroke coincides with the constant angle and falls diagonally – sinister-wise (/).
The thickest stroke falls diagonally – dexter-wise (\), and the two curves are also inclined dexter-wise, and, therefore, in this mode of writing, the stress (i.e. the dominant emphasis of the thickest stroke) is dexter-wise (\), and the two curves, if joined to form an O, make a tilted O.

Now let us try the effect of a different constant angle. Holding the pen shaft straight in front of us (as in figure 23) we get the nib's edge parallel to the writing line, or horizontal. If, with the nib's edge in this position (i.e. constantly parallel with the writing line) we again write the six strokes – the vertical, the horizontal, the two diagonals, and the two full curves – we get the stroke shapes shown in figure 24. In these 'straight-pen' stroke-shapes note especially the following points:
The thinnest stroke coincides with the constant angle and falls horizontally (———).
The thickest stroke falls vertically (I), and the two curves also are upright, and, therefore, in this mode of writing the stress is vertical, and the two curves, if joined to form an O, make an upright O.

93

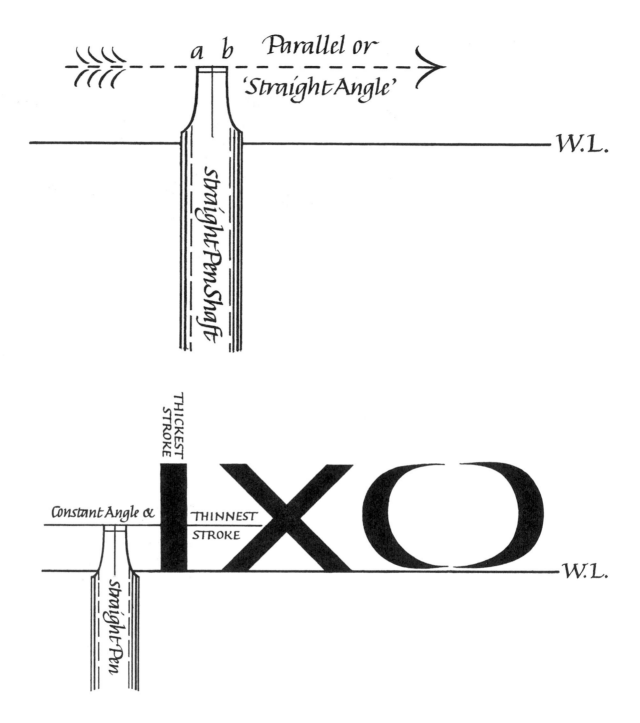

23 (top).Nib's edge (a–b) set parallel to the writing line (W.L.) (compare this with figure 21).
24 (above). The six strokes as shaped by the nib's edge kept parallel to the writing line (i.e. horizontal). Compare this with figure 22.

By comparing figure 22 and figure 24 we may see how either constant angle gives its own characteristic shaping and stressing to every stroke. And it is clear that any two formal manuscripts which differ from each other in their constant angles must differ from each other in every lettter (25).

Note (1): The normal thin stroke, produced by moving the nib edgeways, always coincides with the constant angle of any manuscript. In practice therefore it is convenient to regard the constant angle as the angle of the thin stroke to the writing line. The thin stroke forms a visible and simple clue to the angle, whether we are examining an old manuscript or deciding the precise position on the paper of the edge of our own nib.

25a. Slanted pen writing (constant angle about 35°).

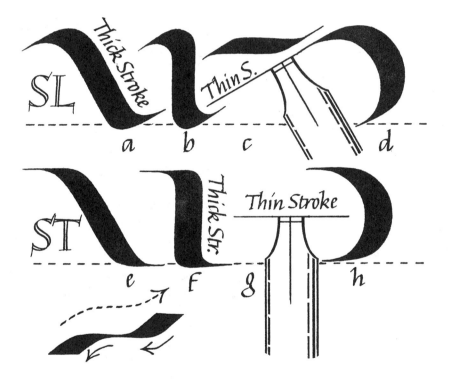

25b. Straight pen writing (constant angle about horizontal).

26. Typical stroke-shapes illustrating two different stresses.
SL = Slanted-pen strokes of 30° stress.
ST = Straight-pen strokes of upright stress.
Note: In changing the stress from 30° in a, b, c, d, to upright in e, f, g, h, a compromise had to be made; while e and f keep the *positions* of a and b they change their breadth shapes, but h keeps its breadth shape and changes the position of d.

Note (2): The two constant angles contrasted in figure 25, like those contrasted in the previous figures, broadly represent two important modes of formal writing, viz., writing which has its thin strokes diagonal (as in writing with a 'slanted pen'), and writing which has its thin strokes approximately horizontal (as in writing with a 'straight pen'). These two modes I have, for many years, distinguished by the rather clumsy but descriptive terms of 'slanted-pen writing' and 'straight-pen writing'.

In order to see the effects of change of stress on our typical stroke-shapes, let us go back again to figure 14 which has a stress of 30°, and – using the original nib, held at the original pen-slant of 30° – copy out its first four stroke-

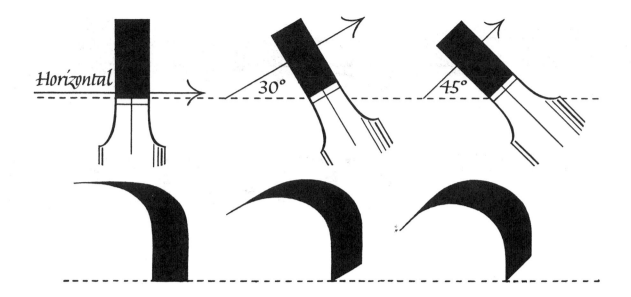

27. Diagram illustrating the differences in stroke incidence and emphasis produced by different constant angles. Observe how, in the three hooked strokes, as the angle is increased, the weight which gives the bias of the stroke is shifted round from the vertical towards the horizontal position, the vertical parts becoming narrower, and the hooks becoming heavier.

shapes which we may call by their *positions* the *dexter* (slant), the *upright*, the *level*, and the *crescent* (tilted) strokes, as in SL, figure 26.

And then, holding the same pen, but this time *straight from the shoulder* so that the stress becomes vertical, let us try to write four strokes as like those of the slanted pen as the straight pen will permit. The nearest copy so made – necessarily a compromise – is seen in ST, figure 26. An experiment will soon show that we have to change shapes, or direction or both.[1]

In the normal use of formal penmanship, in any particular manuscript, the edge of the nib is set, and kept, at a particular angle to the line of writing – i.e., at an angle to the horizontal. This angle is the constant angle, or stress angle, of that particular manuscript, and commonly the most significant pen-factor in its characterization. It decides the incidence of the thin and thick strokes, and, thus, the emphasis, stress, or bias, of the writing.

Different kinds of manuscripts may have different constant angles. For example, the Winchester tenth-century writing which I call the foundational hand has an angle of approximately 30° (as 30° is a good normal angle for the penman, it has been used here in most of the figures illustrating typical elementary pen forms). But some of the earlier manuscripts – especially the rounder and more open hands – are written with the nib's edge nearly horizontal, while some – especially the more compressed hands of the twelfth to sixteenth centuries – have the nib's edge at about 45° to the writing line.

Note: For simplicity of comparison the nib's edges are here shown as square-cut, level, i.e. at right angles to the pen shafts. In practice they would probably be cut, respectively, oblique, slightly oblique and square-cut.

A formal manuscript is directly dominated by the stress of its constant angle in this way. The edge of the writer's nib being held at this chosen angle, it follows that the normal thin stroke – the light edge-stroke of the manuscript – always lies at this angle, and its normal thickest stroke – the heavy width-stroke – lies at right angles to it as in figure 25. A series of strokes of intermediate weights will lie in intermediate positions – between the positions of the thin and the thickest stroke. And the weight (or width) of every stroke is geometrically related to its position in the series.

[1] Note: The pen held differently will give us strokes in similar positions but differing in their weights, breadth-strokes, and strokes having the same shapes but in different positions.

The constant angle settles the position of the whole series in relation to the writing line, and so determines *where* the strokes of given weights shall fall, or *how* strokes of given positions shall be weighted.

Now, in fixing the positions of the heaviest and lightest strokes in manuscript, the constant angle decides exactly upon what part, or parts, of the letters the emphasis shall fall and gives the whole manuscript a directional weight or stress, or bias. And this emphasis falling uniformly throughout a manuscript, together with the exact proportioning of all its strokes according to their positions, gives a special character and striking uniformity and subtle unity to the whole – of which even the untrained, unanalytical eye is sensible.

The letter form

The typical letter form for us is the characteristic structure of any writing which the penman takes for model or pattern. As one of the three primary conditions, it may be described as the *stroke pattern* which the pen has to follow. In its general sense letter form (for every kind of letter maker) means alphabet form, or the typical general plan which distinguishes one alphabet from another.

For example, if we compare the skeleton roman and italic characters in figure 30, we can at once describe their general plan thus: the roman as round-open-upright, and the italic as oval-compressed-sloped. This general distinction of alphabet forms can be carried further by describing other general features – especially constructional features – such as the mode of joining or branching their strokes and the mode of finishing their strokes. For example more complete descriptions of the forms in figure 30 might run thus:

the 'roman' letters are: round-open-upright with high-sprung arch strokes in h, m, r, etc. and added cross-stroke terminals.

the 'italic' letters are: oval-compressed-sloped with low-sprung arch strokes in h, m, r, etc. and natural hook terminals.

Two general features of unique importance in most kinds of lettering are weight and stress. These, the first two factors in penmanship (as described above), are themselves features of the third factor – letter form.

Now, in practice, besides observing the general plan and construction of an alphabet, we must make out – as far as we can – the particular plan and construction of each letter in it. This, for the penman, necessarily involves the shapes of the actual pen-strokes. Therefore his working idea of letter form comprises the shape of every stroke in a given manuscript.

But in formal penmanship (as we have already seen) the shape of every

29. An example of a pen-made letter-form, and its structural tracks, or stroke pattern. The number, order and direction of the tracks is given.

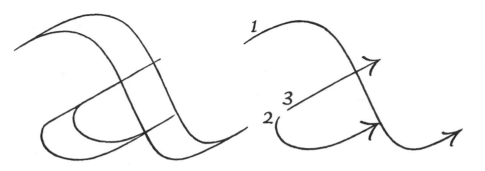

stroke depends on the given weight and constant angle of the nib's edge as it follows the pattern of form. That is to say, by the action of the pen, these three conditions or factors are inseparably combined in the form of the finished manuscript. Therefore the finished manuscript itself is the ultimate and complete letter form.[1]

If we are thinking of copying or creating a special manuscript, we would ordinarily begin with a general idea of the letter-form, then determine the weight and the angle, and then try how to put the strokes together to make the letters we want; and the resulting manuscript is what the pen makes of it. We cannot write a single formal letter without the pen giving (it) weight from its own width, and stress by its own position, while moving and following the stroke-pattern or form. The three factors combine to give us the perfect letter form.

As we have seen, the letter form or pattern which the penman has to follow may already exist on paper, or more or less completely in the penman's mind as an idea, or it may be a pattern in part seen, in part thought, and in part wrought in the very act of writing it. In practice it is necessarily a little of all these three. We think generally of a given alphabet such as any one of these current four: **ABC, abc, *abc*, abc,**

and particularly of a specific variety of any of these alphabets, and ultimately of specific individual letters.

There are innumerable existing patterns or hands, any one of which the penman may choose to copy closely or choose to modify. But as soon as he has decided just what the letter form shall be, that chosen writing pattern becomes the model which he has set himself to follow, and it becomes a conditioning model till that piece of writing is finished.

The practical penman has often made his general choice long before, and he commonly uses one or more hands which have become habitual to him. If he makes any special modification it is likely to be a modification of one or more of his own hands. The principle of a conditioning model remains the same, though by use and habit it will be more perfectly carried out.

But there is a sense in which even his habitual hand becomes a new creation. Here is one of the primary differences between writing and printing. Because even if he habitually uses the same kind of writing, every time he writes he makes it anew, every letter is remade and respaced with his own hand. And when this process of making and remaking by hand is carried out over a long period, there creeps into it a sort of growth and development (largely unconscious).

[1] Using the three factors in copying a manuscript will be found in Chapter 5.

30. Two typical alphabet forms (in skeleton).

these roman small-letters
are round-open-upright

*these italic small-letters
are oval-compressed-sloped*

With practice, the eye becomes truer and more critical, the hand surer and swifter, and this leads almost imperceptibly to instinctive improvement and that maturity and mastery which is only achieved by the gifted scribe after thorough training, steadfast loyalty to principles and years of experience. A manuscript which is continually created and re-created has a life of its own. In printing, compositors are handling ready-made letters – handling, not creating.

We may take the letter O as the clue to the letter-forms of any well-organized alphabet (all the curved or bent forms normally follow the O, and the straight forms have a relative proportion to the O).

The characteristic structure of the O is a clue to the characteristic structure of the alphabet to which it belongs. And a description of the form of the O gives a general description of the letter form of an alphabet.

For a descriptive comparison of the alphabetically different letter forms we may take the characteristic form of the key letter O as representative, and describe it, e.g.

O round and tall

O round and short

O oval and short and sloped

O compressed and angular and short.

Of course the family likeness within an alphabet is helped by all the strokes of any one manuscript being written with the same pen and subject to the same weight and stress.

The typical form of the lettter, or of any family of letters called an alphabet, is literally complete. Besides the framework of the letter, it includes its family construction, and the shaping of its parts by the tool.

The letter form – or the anatomy of letters – is the third of those conditions (or relations between the pen and the letter) which control and produce the characteristic geometrical shapes of formal penmanship.

The two pen conditions give these finished shapes – or formal pen strokes – to the parts of any particular letter form. The anatomy of that letter form gives, or offers, the specific arrangement, size and position of its parts.

ABCDEFGHIJKLM
NOPQRSTUVWXYZ
+ X ◯ [as in TVOP{LY}]

abcdefghijklmnopqrst
uvwxyz from + x o {as in htvo}

ƆEFGᏏLᴍOPRSU
abcdefghijklmnopqrstuvwxyz

31. Rudimentary skeleton forms. Examples of the essential letter forms of Roman capitals and Roman small letters (without stroke finishings, i.e. sanserif). And the six pattern lines or strokes – to which their parts approximate – contributing to their family likeness (note, twenty-two of these skeleton Roman capitals can be made from lines resembling parts of TVO and P, and eighteen of the skeleton small letters from parts of h t v o). For the sake of contrast, two other skeleton letter forms are given – namely, early round forms of capitals (or skeleton uncials) and late compressed forms of small letters (or skeleton italics).

The two pen conditions, (1) the relative position of the nib's edge, and (2) the relative width of the nib, by one movement of the pen, give the stress and weight and the consequent characteristic shape of each stroke of the pen-made letter. But this stress and weight are relative to the position and measure of the strokes, and the particular letter form provides the actual positions and measures. In like manner the whole finished structure of the pen-made letter depends on the structure of its plan. And thus, in so far as a penman follows a given letter form, his writing is conditioned by that form.

Letter forms, in practice, generally exist for us penmen, or are thought of by us, as finished pen-made letters – already developed by other penmen or by ourselves. And whether we copy them, or modify them, or develop new forms from them, it is as finished pen-made letters that we see them, and that we conceive and write our written versions of them.

But, though in practice the forms of the letters we write are inseparable from their pen character, it is sometimes helpful to consider the anatomy of the abstract structural plan of a particular writing. It is convenient to regard such an abstract letter form as though it were an actual skeleton form. And we may consider this skeleton form either, particularly, as the skeleton shape of any one of our letters, or, generally, as the typical family skeleton of any group or alphabet of letters (30 and 31).

Note on group (or alphabet) form. In most of the letters of a normal alphabet we at once recognize a family likeness. This likeness is primarily due to structural similarities in the individual letter forms, commonly to be found in the following four features:

(1) In the special stroke forms (few and repeated) and in the special form or manner of:
(2) the curves (and the internal spacing)
(3) the joinings of the strokes
(4) the finishings of the strokes (not shown in figure 31).

Family likeness, bringing the different letters of any one alphabet (or manuscript, or printer's type) into unison, is one of the chief factors in readableness. Its effective reality may be graphically exemplified thus. If, from a special alphabet, we are given an o and n (or even a single letter d), we can make a fairly good guess at the forms of most of the remaining letters. A more familiar example is found in the ease with which we detect a letter of a wrong fount in a printed page.

In formal penmanship the first test is even more striking. The broad-nibbed pen naturally gives the highest degree of family likeness to the letters written with it, all the strokes of any one alphabet being written with the same pen and subject to the same weight and stress. And the skilled scribe – who allows his pen to help him – can actually produce a surprisingly good conjectural reconstruction of a manuscript of which he has seen only one letter.

Every sort and kind of existing letter forms – whether materially existent or existing in the mind as remembered or pre-imagined forms – are for the penman who writes them the ordered paths, tracks, or directions in which his pen nib has, usually, to travel. And usually – and properly – he follows the structural lines of any hand that he is writing, following with his pen a specified or predetermined track in the correct and usual manner. But he is not bound to follow invariably. What he does is commonly a matter of custom and current legibility, but it is always a matter of choice and of special occasion.

When the occasion justifies it he may play with the forms, or he may even alter the forms to suit the pen. Or, again he may even alter the normal handling of the pen to suit a special letter form. These intentional departures from the conventional course, touch, for the scribe, three of the most interesting aspects of letter form. The student (at least until thoroughly proficient) should limit his study and work to simple stroke writing with a minimum of tricks, comparable to such alphabets as Square Capitals, Uncials, Irish, English and Winchester Hands, but there are very many other aspects of letter form.

The penman's letters consist of these sharply defined, geometrically directional and dimensional stroke shapes, typically finished and typically joined and disposed in vitally structured forms. The basis or plan of such forms is some historic alphabet, past or present or to be (as in a modification of 'tomorrow'), sufficiently like the alphabets now in common use to be readable. Such ancient or modern or future letter forms offer us their typical general disposition of their parts (or strokes), and the individual positions and dimensions, and suggest the mode of spacing, joining, and finishing the parts.

Note: These brief statements on the action of the broad nib are intended to point out particular effects and qualities which are natural to formal penmanship, even in its elements, and to draw the attention of the reader to an essential exactness in the inward parts of our craft. They are but hints at a theory and practice which I myself use, and here proffer for the help of other student penmen in their research. A few words are added below on the *finishing* of pen strokes, and an example of finished pen stroke shapes is given in figure 32.

32. Some examples of the finished, curve-ended, more easily written pen strokes (written here at the common constant angle of 30°). They represent the straight-stemmed, vertical, horizontal, and oblique stroke shapes with natural curve terminations – made with both forward slide and the backward slide of the nib's edge.

Our immediate aim is to understand and to produce good penmanship in which – if we at all succeed – our letters will be vital structures. The individual letter will be something more than a plain putting together of plain strokes. Its strokes will be vitally formed and vitally joined – branched (or grown) out of one another – and their ends will be properly finished: the joined end of a stroke, by the manner of joining it, and the free end, by a suitable special termination.

The special termination of stroke ends is generally so important a feature in a letter that it is commonly identifiable with the letter form itself. In formal penmanship special modes of beginning and ending the strokes are natural and essential to the technique. The particular mode followed is apt to produce a special terminal. If the terminal be part of, and continuous with, the stroke, together they form a new, more complex stroke shape. For example, one of the best modes of starting a stroke, and of stopping it, is to begin and end it with a natural pen curve or 'hook'. Such a hook forms an admirable stroke terminal (and it is so used in many manuscripts). Its effect – made on each end of a straight stroke – is to give the resultant stroke shape a characteristic double wave.[1]

To begin and end the strokes in this way – with curves or hooks – has many advantages, of which the greatest is that it promotes freedom and regularity, by making formal writing easier. It is difficult to write plain straight strokes– like the elementary strokes in figure 11. Especially it is difficult to start them. In fact to enable us to write formal pen strokes with freedom, we must generally start with a preliminary edgeways movement of the nib – a short slide of the nib's edge, forward or back. And to end the stroke with a final edgeways movement, though less generally necessary, is very helpful to the writer. The curve finish naturally begins and ends a stroke with this helpful edge movement.

This curve-finishing helps and enhances the penmanship (among other things it introduces the characteristic contrast of thick and thin). It naturally perfects the elementary stroke shapes and gives them a vitality of their own. It may be seen how curved or crescent strokes similarly make their own perfect endings, but the plain, straight elements there are like basic crystals which the pen's magic here turns into living things.

[1] See *The Imprint*, figure 28. E.J. intended to develop in F.P. the special ways of beginning and ending letter-strokes. Some pen-stroke terminals are indicated in his Alphabet class-sheet, Plate 14. *Ed.*

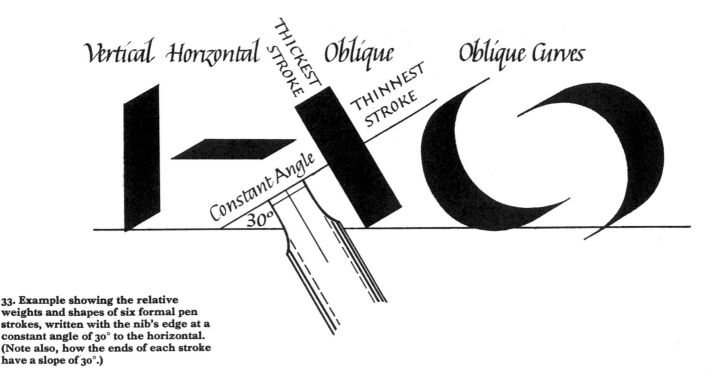

33. Example showing the relative weights and shapes of six formal pen strokes, written with the nib's edge at a constant angle of 30° to the horizontal. (Note also, how the ends of each stroke have a slope of 30°.)

Summing-up

It is clear then, that, in any given ideal formal manuscript, the stress of the relative widths, and the patch-like (or ribbon-like) shapes, of our pen strokes depend on the relative positions or directions in which these strokes lie, and on the movement of the broad nib's edge – of a set width and maintained at a constant angle – along or through these directions (28). Normally we use little or no pressure. Normally we move the pen in a steady almost mechanical manner. Normally we obey, or follow, the pen. And, though we choose for ourselves (or, rather, *set* ourselves) many different conditions – such as the letter form and the particular constant angle, size, weight, colour, arrangement, etc. – and, though we specially fashion, or hold the pen to accord with our conditions, and, though we 'play' with writing, and, though we make the whole writing conform to our intention, yet it is true to say of our written manuscript that all the normal and mechanical effects of thicks and thins, of contrast and harmony, of structural uniformity or (where we use more than one hand) variety, in it, have come naturally and, in the main, are given to us by our formal broad nib.

Chapter 4   Experiments with twin points

To the practical reader: take two pencils; put them side by side, with the points level; fasten the pair firmly together – at each end – with fine string ties, or tightly lapped rubber bands.

These double-pencils, or twin points, are an excellent tool for demonstrating the natural effects of the broad nib. The two points of the pencils act like the two sharp corners of the nib, and give us – in a sort of 'parallel' or duplicate outline – very nearly the characteristic forms or shapes of formal penmanship (34).

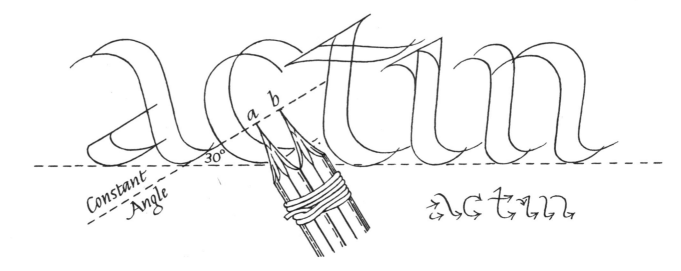

34. Twin-points acting like a broad nib, and the characteristic 'pen forms' produced by them. (The small skeletons show the various paths of the strokes.)

Note: The student can copy this, if he sets his double-pencils exactly as shown, and keeps them at this slant throughout the writing of every stroke.

The two points (a and b) form the 'nib' of this skeleton 'pen'. In comparing its double skeleton, or hollow strokes, with the inked, or solid strokes of the true pen, we find that the outlines of the hollow one, and the edges of the other solid one, correspond exactly – save in one small detail. The twin-points 'nib' produces a small external 'dimple' at the ends, and end-junctions, of its curved strokes. Whereas, with real pen strokes, the inky edge of the nib bridges across, and fills, this 'dimple' – making, at that point, a slight thickening and a flatness in the outer curve (35).

There is another difference in the outline of the 'hollow' strokes, which is possible, but it does not affect the 'shape' of the contained space. Twin-points will make plain straight strokes consisting of two parallel lines not joined

35. Twin-point strokes (showing the external 'dimples', xxxx, at the curve ends) compared with true pen strokes (showing the slight external thickening and flattening / / / /, at the curve ends).

anywhere – that is, they will make open-ended straight strokes. Plain straight strokes, however, rarely occur in actual writing, either with the pen or with the twin-points, for nearly all strokes are curved, or otherwise finished, at the ends (the 'dot' of the twin-point i may show open-ended, or partly so, as in figure 35).

In all other respects the shapes of the strokes, made by the pen and by the double-pencils, are the same. And even in the matter of the 'dimple', the true pen actually has, in practice, a tendency to make these 'dimples'. In short, the twin-points give a faithful representation of true pen characters – plus an instructive emphasis on the vitally important effects and tendencies of the pen nib's corners.

Twin-points have a special value in the analytical study of formal manuscript, for they reveal the principles and the internal anatomy of a letter, where, in pen writing, the ink would be apt to conceal them (the thin lines internally crossing the thick stems of a and n – figure 34, exemplify this).

The double-pencils will also help the beginner over the technical difficulties of obtaining true pen shapes. At first the real nib is more difficult to handle truly, and the pen itself – by unskilful use, blurring and concealing the true shapes – is apt to confuse him as to right and wrong pen effects, and yet to flatter him with its glamour.

The twin-points 'nib' is comparatively free from difficulty and ambiguity, and it will show him very nearly, diagrammatically and clearly, what it is that the properly used pen actually does.

I advise every student of formal penmanship, therefore, to begin with double-pencils. He will find that a very little time spent in experimenting with them will give him a clear conception of formal pen shapes, to start with, and a criterion by which he can presently judge his early pen and ink work.

Now, take a piece of any smooth unglazed paper, and, with your double-pencils, experiment, and find out what various shapes you will get if you move the twin-points 'nib' in various directions on its surface. A pad (such as a section of blotting paper, or an ordinary magazine) laid under the writing paper will help you to keep both points touching it.

To use a metaphor, which though 'mixed' is yet most apt – as will be shown later – try your hand at fancy skating. Take the two ordinary pencils, with their string ties (or rubber bands), for a trial 'run' – as I have done in figure 36. Vary the experiment as you please, but hold the 'shaft' at the same pen slant throughout, looking only for that variety in the double track made by the twin-points that comes from moving them through different and changing directions, while their own direction (or constant angle) remains unchanged.

Note: The pencils were held throughout at the set slant indicated here; they therefore produced the thinnest strokes in the direction of the arrow, and the thickest strokes at right angles to the arrow.

The arrow in fact represents the constant angle of this writing – which is 30°. And to give the twin-points 'nib' this inclination of 30° to the horizontal the shaft of the pencils is held at a slant of 30° to the perpendicular. The student can repeat the experiment, setting himself other constant angles.

A note on the keeping of the constant angle of a writing

All that is required of the scribe is that he should keep the nib's edge constantly in close approximation to its proper position. Until it becomes a habit, he must consciously beware of straying from it. One does not alter the slant when writing naturally. Students are apt to follow the fancy skating shapes anyhow of volition rather than allow the shapes to be produced by the natural action of the pen.

It may help you occasionally to watch the slant at which you are holding the shaft of the pencils (or the pen), and to see that you are not altering it from the particular slant which gives the required constant angle of the nib. But, normally, the eyes must be kept on the nib itself and on what it is doing – that is, when learning, we closely observe the correct placing (and maintaining) of the edge of the nib, and note its effects on weight and shape and structure.

When making studies of a writing, it is very helpful first to mark your exercise paper repeatedly with the correct constant angle of the writing.

For the present copies: take some ruled paper, or rule some lines, about 1 inch apart, for writing on. Then cut a triangular piece of card or paper having an angle of 30° (you can get this angle from figure 37). With this card angle, used as a protractor, draw this constant angle at the beginning of each writing line (as in figure 38), or even at the beginning of each stroke (as in figure 38).[1]

When copying, begin by placing both points of the double-pencils upon this constant angle line, and, while you write, try to keep them at that angle – just as you would place and keep the edge of the nib of a real pen (4). First: copy the 'hollow' o and i in figure 35, and note how the twin-points produce 'dimples' at the curve ends. Copy the 'hollow' letters (actin) in figure 34, and note their structure – especially noting their internal structure. Now, try to imitate the 'solid' pen and ink strokes (which follow) with your 'hollow' twin-point strokes.

Rule an angle line for the beginning of each stroke (as in figure 37). Begin each stroke in this way: upon this angle line (as in figure 37), place the two pencil points. Regard them as though they were the two corners of the nib as shown in figure 33, and, keeping their angular position unchanged, draw them in the proper direction – for each stroke, respectively.

In making the six strokes of figure 33 the nib moves:

Vertically – Downwards
Horizontally – Forwards
Thin obliquely – Forward-Upward
Thick obliquely – Downward-Forward
Left hand curve – from Backward-Downward 'round' to Forward-Up
Right hand curve – from Forward-Upward 'round' to Backward-Down

[1] The smaller angle of a 60° set-square is 30° and it is useful for the purpose described by E.J. *Ed.*

36. 'Fancy skating' with double-pencils: illustrating the varying widths and (ribbon-like) shapes of their tracks, caused by the varying *directions* of those tracks.

For the four straight strokes in this test (as was done in the original of figure 33) use a flat ruler, or any straight edge, to guide the tool movement accurately – Vertically, Horizontally, and Obliquely. For the two curved strokes 'write' in free-hand (or, on transparent paper, trace them with the double-pencils from figure 33).

Note: As the width of the double-pencils 'nib' is about half the width of the pen nib employed in figure 33, so the present strokes have been made about half the length of the originals in order to preserve their relative weights-and-shapes.

Observe that the plain straight strokes – the Vertical, Horizontal, and Thick-Oblique – though left open-ended by the double pencils, contain the same shapes as the pen strokes in figure 33.

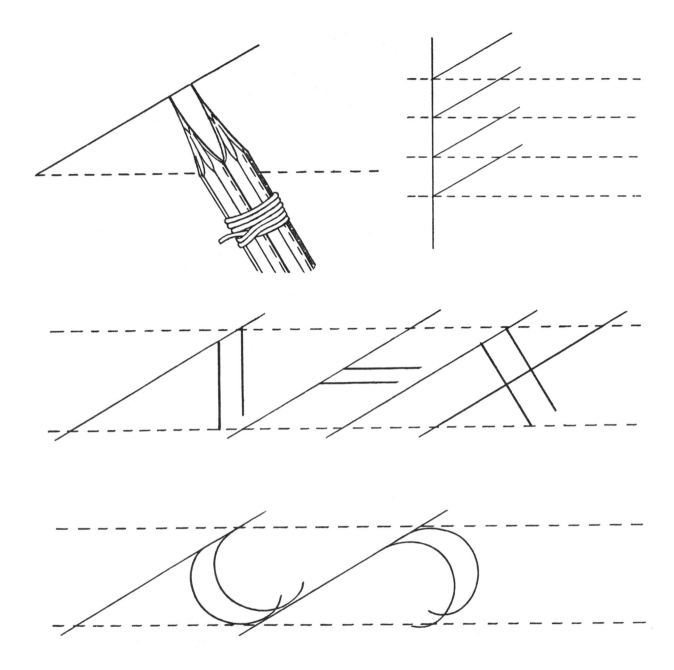

37 (top). Ruled writing line (i.e. the 'horizontal') with ruled constant angle line (here at 30°), and the twin-points in position for copying. 38 (above). The six formal pen strokes of figure 33 copied or imitated in twin-point strokes. To assist in preserving the constant angle of these strokes (which is 30°) each stroke has been started from a previously ruled line.

If you have made these strokes accurately, a straight line (or edge of paper) laid across their open ends will show that their end-slopes agree with the slope of the constant angle.

Check the truth of the statements which precede figure 33 in regard to the weights and shapes of any given pen strokes being dependent upon the position of the nib's edge and the directions in which the strokes lie.

Note: The letters in figure 25,a and in figure 25,b have been written with a pen nib about half the width of your double-pencils 'nib'. In the proportional size, imitate the 'outlines' of figure 28 and note how the emphatic regular fall of the heavy stroke – especially along the tops, or 'shoulders', and along the 'feet' of the letters – gives uniformity to the line of writing. You may bring out this effect, by 'shading' the thickest parts after they are written.

39. Example of copying writing with a wider 'nib'.
Original   Pen nib is about ⅛ inch wide.
             Pen letter is about ½ inch high.
Copying   Twin-point 'nib' is about ¼ inch wide.
             Twin-point letter is about 1 inch high.

Note: In imitating the outlines of the letters in figure 28 your thick strokes will be about twice the width of theirs. Keep the right proportion, by making your letters about twice the linear size of their letters (39). Draw the skeleton forms and letters of figure 3 with a single pencil – about twice their present height and width – and rewrite them with the double-pencils.

The student is now in a position to appreciate the very brief initial statement of what the formal pen makes and how it works. Practical experience is necessary to the student in order that he may, from the first, see and feel for himself, and have explicit knowledge of the ideal normal action of the formal pen. For a little actual handling of the pen or of the skeleton pen, formed by our twin-points, which so admirably reflects its action – gives a clearer and truer knowledge of formal penmanship than many chapters of description.

Note: The student need neither be discouraged nor too pleased (though that is rarer) by the appearance of his attempts at writing when his practice and knowledge are still small. Some awkwardness in using a new tool and some inaccuracy in early copying are inevitable. But the truth of the matter can be seen through these faults and limitations – seen in spite of them, or even because of them.

What concerns the student who has to proceed from small beginnings is that we should have our little knowledge early, know it to be true, and grasp it clearly. Such knowledge will grow and grow aright.

To this end, the student is advised to follow or check most of my technical statements in this book, as he comes to them, by brief practical trials in passing, either with a formal pen and ink or with twin-points.

When he is actually learning to write, and later in advanced studies of manuscript, pen and ink are, of course, essential. And, as a penman, he must always have by him a good pen and proper ink, both ready for use, as ready as possible.

But nearly all questions of pen form can be graphically and instructively demonstrated – sometimes with advantage – by the twin-points. And this and the simplicity and convenience of this tool make it desirable and possible that the student should always have it beside him, ready to experiment with, whether he is reading this book or studying or planning manuscripts.

The general reader also, or anyone interested in formal penmanship, may easily assist his apprehension of the matter by accompanying his reading or studies with brief practical experiments with double-pencils.

As this tool is to be our constant companion, we had better try to improve it and make it as handy as possible. The width of two ordinary pencils is a little awkward both for holding and for ordinary use, and the fixed ties interfere with proper adjustment of the points. The improvement of the double-pencils in these respects – by planing away some of the wood of the pencils, and by butting them in a metal sleeve – is described in the Chapter on Tools.[1]

These things might tax the reader's skill too much, and would, in this place, unduly interrupt our theme. But we can at once make a substitute for the most important of them – that is a tightly fitting 'sleeve' which holds the two pencils together (without tying) and yet permits either pencil to be slid forward or back, for adjustment or re-sharpening. A very good substitute 'sleeve' can be made by anyone, in ten minutes or so, with a stout postcard and a piece of string.

Wrap about 3 inches of the card around the double-pencils (between the two original ties) and whip the card tightly, but not too tightly, with fine string, whipping as shown below. Then remove the two original ties (40). Either pencil, when its end is pressed, should slide smoothly against the other, but without any slipping.

40. Double-pencils fitted with card 'sleeve'.

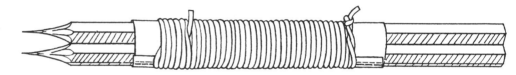

Note: The quickest and simplest way of making it possible to slide either pencil forward or back (without untying the pair) is to use rubber bands for holding the pair together. Either pencil can then be slid by adjusting the bands. But the necessary tightness and the 'pull' of the bands make nice adjustment of the points rather difficult. Still this is a possible, temporary makeshift, and better than having the pencils not slidable.

The chief object in having the pencils slidable in our skeleton pen is to permit easy and exact adjustment of the line of the two points (which constitutes the 'nib') – just as, in the true pen, we adjust the line of the edge of the nib – making it level or oblique.

The nib's edge, in the true pen, is adjusted by cutting or grinding it. The twin-point 'nib' is adjusted by sliding one of its points forward or back. In either case this adjustment determines the angle of the nib – i.e. the angle of the nib's edge to the shaft (41). The chief effect of changing the angle of a nib is to change the relation between the direction of its thin stroke and the 'slant' of the pen shaft. It may be changed primarily to fit the nib for writing a particular manuscript, or primarily for the comfort of the penman.

The angle of a nib may be changed then in order to allow the writer to hold the shaft of the pen at the slant which he finds comfortable – without departing from the constant angle of the particular manuscript which he is writing.

For example, in figures 34, 35 and 36, the constant angle of the nib's edge has been set at 30° to the horizontal. Now, if the points of the twin-points be

[1] This chapter does not appear to exist. *Ed.*

41. True pen nibs and twin-point 'nibs' having two different angles namely, level and oblique.

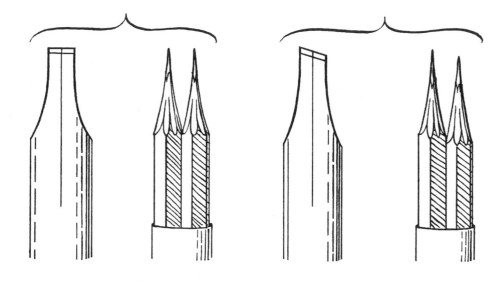

level, the shaft must be held by the writer at the constant slant of 30° (to the perpendicular). But if a particular writer should find it more comfortable to hold the shaft at a greater slant – say, at 45° – he can still keep the original constant angle (30°) of the writing by a slight adjustment of the points. Actually he would push the left-hand pencil slightly forward (or, alternatively, slide the right-hand pencil slightly back), so altering the angle of his twin-points 'nib' and making it slightly oblique (42). Or if, for any reason, a writer prefers a less slanted pen, a slight obliquity of the nib, to the left, will allow for it.

Such compensatory adjustments of the nib will allow the penman a considerable choice of pen slants – within a range, say, of about 30° for the more common formal manuscripts. For example, with manuscripts having a constant angle of 30° the penman may choose any slant of his pen shaft between 15° and 45° from the perpendicular.

The limitations of the pen slant are primarily due to the desirable limitations of the nib's angle. A reasonable limit for the nib's angle is about 15° of obliquity. (Note: In figure 10 the oblique nibs are shown with this limit of obliquity.)

Note: Among the minor effects produced by changing the angle of the nib – from the square-cut to the oblique – there are two which may be noted here in passing:

(1) An oblique-edged nib makes the pen shaft roll over slightly in the direction of the slope of the obliquity.

(2) With a given cross width of nib (as in double-pencils) an oblique edge is slightly wider (between the points) than a level edge and therefore makes slightly wider strokes. These things will be dealt with later.

Much has been said above (and some of it, I trust, has already been proved by the reader) of the use of twin-points in studying pen forms. As the skeleton to the living form, so does the work of this skeleton pen draw our attention – in some ways more strikingly than the pen itself – to the salient features of formal penmanship.

The double-pencils are easy to prepare – pencils and string can be found anywhere – and their handiness and convenience add greatly to their value. They can be carried in the pocket, kept in the hand while reading or studying,

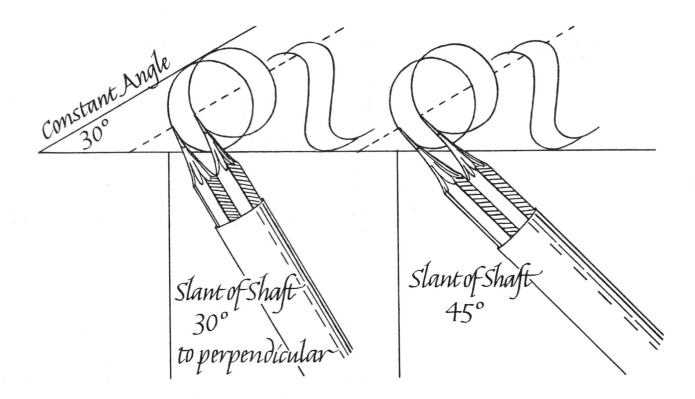

42. The same constant angle of a writing (e.g. 30°) may be kept by twin-points (or pens) though held at different slants, when the 'nibs' have suitably adjusted angles. Here are two twin-point 'pens': Twin-point with level 'nib' held at a slant of 30° to perpendicular: Twin-point with oblique 'nib' held at a slant of 45° to perpendicular but both giving the same constant angle for the manuscript of 30°.

and used more easily (and safely) than a pen, in almost any place or position – for example, on any sort of table (without a desk), and on any markable, smooth material, in a notebook, on a wall, etc. Besides their use in preliminary studying, there are other uses for which they are especially apt by their quick and simple use (a perfect pen, skilfully used, will do all the better, but takes more care and time):

(1) For experimental drafts of manuscripts. In experimental planning or designing of certain letter varieties, and in the designing or drawing of certain exact and measured letters, such as block letters.

Note: Other craftsmen – such as stone or wood carvers – would find them useful for such planning, and also for making preliminary drafts or sketches for inscriptions, either for their own use or to be shown to clients.

(2) In teaching students they are useful to both master and pupil. For this purpose, besides the plain double-pencils, tied or sliding, a valuable variety is a couple of pencils – especially of differently coloured pencils – red and black – simply held in the hand.

Transformed into two chalks – either plain, or in two colours – simply held in the hand, or in a special holder, they are useful for blackboard demonstrations.

Chapter 5   Using the three factors in copying a manuscript

Although in practice (as explained in Chapter 3) complete letter form is inseparable from weight and angle and stress, yet it is at times very helpful to use these three factors analytically, and it is almost essential when we are copying a manuscript.

For example, let us suppose that we are about to copy the special manuscript forms of E, O, and S, in figure 43.

43. Some fourteenth-century English Manuscript capitals (written large).

The weight of these letters must first be found (44). Beginning our copying with the letter O, we measure the width of its thick stroke. Finding that this is exactly a ¼ inch (at the broadest part: a–b in figure 44), we take a ¼-inch pen for writing the copy.

We then measure the height of the letters. Finding that they are about an inch – or four nib-widths – high, we rule the copying paper with some light pencil lines 1 inch apart.

44. The weight is given by the ratio width of thick stroke (a–b) to height of letter (c–d).

The constant angle: we must next find the angle which the thin stroke (in the manuscript) makes with the writing line (45). This angle appears to be about 37°. We therefore slant our ¼-inch pen so that the nib's edge makes this angle, or rather approximates sufficiently nearly to it, with the ruled lines of the copying paper, and (having inked it) we slide the nib edge sideways from a lower to an upper ruled line. This slide, properly made, will give a thin stroke like that of the O in the manuscript.

45. The constant angle is given by the thin stroke of the manuscript.

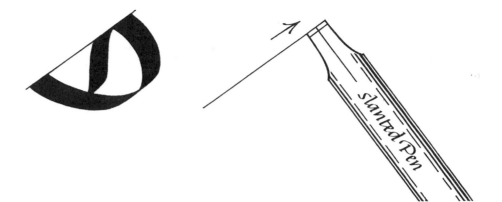

When we are able to repeat this thin stroke naturally, still keeping the nib's edge at the proper constant **angle**, we can copy the four component strokes of this manuscript O (46).

46. The manuscript O and its four component strokes.

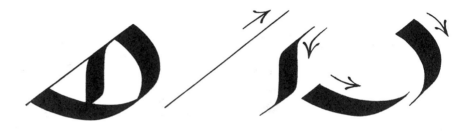

We have now to find out how these component strokes are put together to form the O. It introduces three secondary factors of penmanship, namely, the number, the order, and direction of strokes; that is to say, the number of strokes and the order and direction in which they are made in any given letter.

As this aspect of construction is important in copying and has an important bearing upon letter form, a few notes on the method of making up the E, O and S are given here.

The strokes of the O were probably put together as shown in figure 47.

47. Construction of the manuscript O.

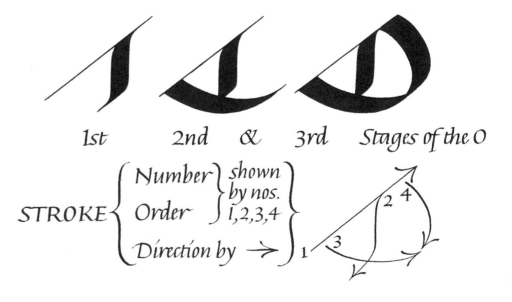

1st   2nd   &   3rd   *Stages of the O*

STROKE { Number } shown by nos. 1,2,3,4 } Order } Direction by →

In making the E we see an interesting constructional feature. It seems to have been made exactly as the O was made up to the second stage, and then a double stroke (like a 2) was added to it and the E was complete (48). As to

48. Construction of the manuscript E.

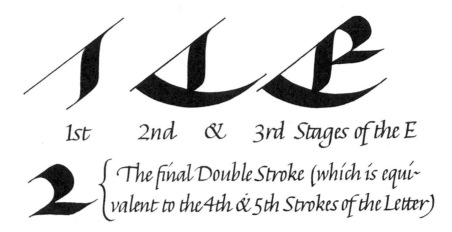

1st   2nd   &   3rd Stages of the E

2 { The final Double Stroke (which is equi-
{ valent to the 4th & 5th Strokes of the Letter)

the construction of the S it is probable that its main, or serpentine, stroke was made first and its thin stroke second. We may perhaps guess the order of making the other strokes, as – the upper arm third, and the lower arm last.

The direction in which all these strokes are made is, of course, mainly forward – from left to right.

We may note in passing that two of the strokes of the S (viz., the second and third) nearly resemble the first and third of the O.

49. Construction of the manuscript S.

Let us now suppose that we have copied these manuscript letters, and let us take the last six figures (44 to 49), as representing our method of copying. It can be seen that in these figures we have made the first three strokes of the O and the E and at least nine times (and over) – with very marked uniformity. This uniformity of stroke shapes is mainly due to our having preserved the proper weight and angle of the manuscript and to preserve the weight and angle is the best way to preserve the letter form.

The letter form of this particular manuscript is described here from what we find in the three sample capitals, E, O, and S in figure 43. We now note – besides their actual weight and stress –

their strong Gothic character;

their long, heavy, forward-sweeping curves;

their long, up-and-forward-sliding thin strokes;

and the sharp contrast of their thick and thin strokes accentuated by their angular stroke joinings.

Some of this we must have felt or seen beforehand – when we chose the manuscript for copying – but all of it becomes clear and much more dawns upon us when we actually write these letters. As our copying progresses there are hints of great possible speed – without loss of form.

We glimpse, indeed, in these letters the three essential virtues; they are very free, and also formal, and they have a structural and constructional unity which shows in a strong family likeness.

With the pen in our hand we half realize how letter forms such as these must have been first created, how they must have grown and developed, how essentially they are products of the formal pen – and, if we watch, they will give us hints of what the pen likes to do.

The ancient scribe played his creative part. The modern man with the pen still may play his. He may even, to a great extent, choose the three conditions. And the pen will dominate the result – as the tool does in all good workmanship.

To sum up – the very act of writing brings all three conditions, weight, angle and form, into play mutually, conditioning any manuscript which is being written. The reader is strongly urged to take two common pencils and some scribbling paper, and, with these, to make a practical acquaintance with pen forms.

Chapter 6 The use of the formal pen: pen stroke 'constants' or the seven rules for copying a manuscript

Résumé of the qualities of formal pen strokes

We have learnt something of the normal action of the formal pen, and (it is assumed) have proved it with the skeleton pen. By writing simple pen strokes we have seen how the pen makes the strokes – shaping and weighting them in (theoretically) absolute relation to the direction in which the nib's edge moves. And we have seen that, as in writing a particular manuscript, the nib's edge is always set and kept at a (particular) constant angle to the horizontal, and this shaping and weighting of the strokes in a particular manuscript depends, in practice, on the directions in which its strokes lie. And thus all the parts of its strokes which lie in the same directions have the same shapes and weights.

We have seen also that the harmony of this relation – of shape and weight with nib-and-stroke-direction – gives a characteristic uniformity to the writing, while at the same time it produces a characteristic (and, often, striking) contrast between the thick and the thin strokes.

And (in such experiments as are suggested in figure 36) we must also have found or felt in this pen something – almost a tendency to make, certainly a natural swiftness of movement and a special aptness in the pen, for making easy running ribbon-like strokes and, even, flourishes – which may be called natural or controlled freedom.

In short, we have seen that the formal broad-nibbed pen, by its faculty for making geometrically related strokes and by its natural movements, produces highly formal characters having uniformity, harmony, contrast and freedom. These natural qualities of our writing will be discussed further, but here I shall sum them all up by saying that, in its essential character, formal penmanship has three fundamental qualities or first principles –

Sharpness
Unity
Freedom

The fundamental technique and the three essential characteristics

In order to understand the ideal action of the formal pen we must now look more fully into the use or technique of the formal pen, and consider what the penman actually does – when he is writing a formal manuscript.

Firstly, it is necessary to remind the student that to obtain the forms of pen letters, the true contrasts of their thicks and thins, the written strokes must be clean-cut and sharp, and that to produce such strokes the nib's edge must be true – sharp-edged and sharp-cornered – and must touch the writing surface (vellum, parchment, or paper) truly and equally with both its corners. And, to maintain the FORM of a particular manuscript, and the uniformity of its writing, we must keep the shape and width of the nib, and the position of its edge (or constant angle), as set for that manuscript, unchanged. That is, briefly stated, throughout any given piece of writing, we keep to the same, or similar, nib, and we hold it in the same manner. The nib may become blunt and require recutting or renewing, but the new nib must be fashioned and held exactly like the old one.

At first the student can neither cut nor resharpen a pen perfectly nor set it down on the paper with such sureness that both its sharp corners (if they are sharp) are in contrast with the surface. But nevertheless, he can, from the first, by careful examination, distinguish between true pen strokes and faulty ones.

A practical application of the first three principles should help his discrimination. He will find that the trueness of pen strokes shows itself in three characteristics; the strokes are:

Sharp-edged

Uniformly made

and Swift.

These three essential characteristics represent the fundamental technique of the formal penman and also – it may be truly said – the beginning and the end of formal penmanship.

Here, then, is a brief restatement of the practical means by which the penman can make sure that his writing shall have the three essential characteristics:

Efficient tools and true contact	Efficient pens, inks and writing surfaces, and true contact of the nib and the surface, will give the edges of the strokes sharp definition.
Keeping the nib true and its position constant	Maintaining the condition of the nib's edge, and its position (or constant angle) will give the strokes the uniformity of relative weighting and shaping.
Writing Making Creating MSS	Finally, practice in writing promotes the control of hand and pen which will give the strokes sureness-and-freedom of direction-and-movement.

Let the penman remember these three essential things!

A note on the pens and ink to be used now by the practical reader

When the necessary knowledge and experience have been gained, the proper tools of our craft – pens, ink and other writing materials – will be found to be both simple and easy to use. But, in the meantime, tools with more exaggerated features will demonstrate the essential things more clearly. Very wide pen nibs and very thin ink, or the skeleton pen (the double-pencils), by their exaggeration of the fundamental technique, enable a beginner (or a scribe who has overlooked these essentials) to see and to make true pen strokes for himself.

After the student has been helped by that experience, by some practice with these large tools, and he begins to use the normal tools (the less wide nibs and the thicker inks) of the scribe, he will more readily see what is faulty in his penwork and he will also know better what technical perfection to seek for.

Note: Here are some of the advantages that double-pencils have for a beginner who has not yet learnt to cut (or grind) a pen nib accurately, or to touch his writing paper truly with its edge. With the double-pencils 'nib', the theoretical 'edge' – being the 'line' joining the two points – is almost geometrically true. Its two 'corners' are the points themselves, and they are as sharp as the pencils are pointed. And the act of setting this skeleton pen to paper, so that both its points touch the writing surface, is much easier, for the unpractised hand and eye, than the placing of a real pen nib's edge in true contact with the paper.

For the pen and ink copying, the beginner (if he cannot get a proper pen) may try one of the large flat metal writing tools – not less than a $\frac{1}{4}$ inch wide – and common thin writing ink, or stick indian ink much diluted. A thin writing fluid is easiest for the beginner's use. On ordinary paper it will give fairly sharp-edged strokes (should the paper be slightly porous, a few drops of gum may be added to the ink to prevent it from spreading).

As the student of formal penmanship must learn eventually how to make and use a pen, he will do better still if he can now cut a real pen of hollow hard cane, with a sufficiently accurate nib (a good cane pen makes the best tool that I know for large writing; figures 43–49 were written with a small piece of bamboo – originally a garden stake). The nib should be about $\frac{3}{16}$ inch wide. If he cannot at first cut such a pen for himself, he may perhaps find another scribe who will cut one for him. In that case, however, he must learn to re-sharpen it for himself. A reasonably sharp pen nib is indispensable for formal penmanship.

Pen stroke 'constants' or the seven rules for copying a manuscript

These rules apply to the production of any type of formal penmanship; they may therefore be thought of as the seven rules for writing. By keeping them, as well as he can, the penman may be reasonably sure of producing a formal writing which is true to the desired type.

Any given writing has its own type of letter – that is, its own variety of the alphabet. And, for the sake of readableness and beauty and the use of the pen, there must be a family likeness throughout the letters of the alphabet. To give, or preserve, this special likeness, the technique must be kept constant throughout a given writing.

Different writings have different 'constants'. It is in fact the 'constants' in any one writing which give it its special character.

The seven rules deal with seven important constant elements in pen technique. These constant elements are the special ways of making and combining pen strokes to form a special writing or 'hand'. They may therefore be appropriately termed 'pen stroke constants'.

The function of the seven rules is to help the penman, or the student of penmanship, to preserve the essential family likeness or character of any particular kind or variety of the alphabet, as it appears in the particular formal

50. A table of the seven constant features which distinguish manuscripts.

N.B. The examples given in the third column, are from a particular hand (viz., 'The foundational hand', figure 18) and show its distinctive constant features. Any other type of hand would show its own characteristics, differing from the above examples in some or all of the seven features.

Pen stroke 'constants'

Features normally constant in any manuscript The 7 features	Definitions of features	Examples from a special hand (the MS of figure 18)
Three features which determine the character of the writing		
'Angle' of MS	The angle at which the nib's edge is set – relatively to the horizontal line of the writing	In this particular hand the angle = approx. 30°
'Weight' of MS	The width of the thick stroke of the letters in relation to their height. (This ratio is conveniently inverted as letter-height to nib-width: e.g. LH = abt. 4 × NW.)	Its 'stem' or nib-width is approx. ¼ of height of letters (o, a, & c.)
'Shape' of MS	Briefly, the curve of the curved strokes, and the finishes of the straight strokes (commonly set, by the o & the i, for the rest)	Its (mean) o is approx. circular: its i is headed & hooked.
Three features affecting the construction of the letters		
Number of strokes	The number of separately made strokes (in each letter)	In its a (e.g.) there are three separate strokes
Order of strokes	The order in which the strokes are written (in each letter)	1st 2nd 3rd
Pen-direction in strokes	The direction in which the pen nib travels in making each separate stroke (commonly downwards & forwards, with short edge sliding up).	indicates path of pen
The modifying features of speed		
Speed of writing	The proper rate for each movement of the pen, or the actual speed of the scribe in writing the original MS or copy.	(e.g.) Overshot last stroke indicates rapid writing

hand to which it belongs. It is equally true, and it reveals a more vital aspect of the rules, to say that their function is to help the penman to give to each and all of his different writings their different proper family likenesses. And their immediate purpose, at this point, is to help the student to see, definitely, the elements or features which constitute these family likenesses in formal penmanship.

When we consider further what the penman is actually doing when he writes a formal hand, we shall find that there is something, in the act of writing, which is essentially of the nature of copying. Briefly put, the writer – whether imitating a manuscript, or writing professionally, or inventing letter forms – is following a material, or habitual, or imagined model of the alphabet. And, moreover, in a given piece of writing (though he may, within limits, subtly modify or improve upon his real or ideal model) he is bound by the character, both of what he has already written and of what he intends to write. He is bound, that is, to follow and preserve the general family likeness of that writing by relating each letter of it to all its other letters.

It is therefore most convenient to present these rules as rules for copying a manuscript. Though it must be understood that that manuscript may be actual or imagined, and that it is really its true likeness which we copy. The seven features of any hand (of Latin or Western derivation) which the penman tries to 'copy' – or, rather, does his best to see and preserve or give – are set out in the table opposite, figure 50. This table is illustrated by examples from the foundational hand (18). Examples from any other type of *hand* would differ from these, in some or all of the seven features, as one family or tribe differs from another.

The value and uses of the formal pen

In the above general statement of its virtues, effects and uses, the formal broad-nibbed pen has been described as the special tool by which the craft of formal penmanship exists.

Its working virtue has been shown to be a faculty for producing highly formal and free characters, and a harmony of parts which approaches unity. And it may be seen that these geometrically shaped 'parts' or strokes, which it almost automatically produces, aptly and naturally make up into the conventional, finished shapes of our ordinary letters.

But, these ordinary letters have come down to us from the broad-nibbed pen of the ancient penman. And herein, for us, lies that same pen's fundamental value. It is the primary shaper and maker of our letter forms – and it can shape still that which its own shape has made.

For over 1000 years (between AD 400 and 1500) the broad nib was the principal formative tool in the development of writing. From the early, stylus-made skeleton letters, it produced the conventional finished shapes and varieties which we now use (familiar to most of us mainly in print). The finished shape-and-structure of the common alphabet is, in fact, bound up with the shape-and-action of our pen.

This pre-eminently letter-making tool has many uses for the modern formal penman. And some of these uses would be of value to all who make or study 'lettering'. Not only penmen, but most handicraftsmen, and even students of palaeography, will find the broad nib valuable for copying, for examining (or detecting), for modifying, and for matching (or recovering) old or existing letter forms, and for suggesting or inventing new ones.

Note: These and other uses of the broad nib are summarized below.

Copying

Copies of any manuscript forms of text, or capitals, or initials – originally written with a broad nib – can be almost perfectly made by skilled present-day penmen. Even a student little practised in writing will discover the indispensable help that the pen will give him – if he will allow it to – in making a copy.

Examining or detecting

Experiments with the pen will help greatly in examining or finding out the actual structure of any formal manuscript which must precede copying. They will even throw light on other than pen-made forms: e.g. the 'faces' of early printers' types may sometimes be very nearly made out, in this way. The pen has been responsible for, or has influenced, the structure of many kinds of letters including all our small letters (even the shapes of the early capital letters in incised inscriptions in stone may have been affected by it). It may therefore be appealed to – by practical experiment – as a sort of authority on the actual structure of many ancient letters, and similarly, it may be appealed to on the question of the proper construction of modern letters based on early forms. In short, it may be 'consulted' as an authority on orthodox letter shape.

Modifying

The pen may be used to modify any other pen forms – old or new. One may in this way substitute harmonious modern features for archaic features (and see Matching, below), or one may change the fashion of any manuscript in any desired direction. Either process is carried out by the pen appropriately and characteristically.

Matching or recovering

The broad nib will also supply letters which are wanting, absent, or damaged, in a manuscript which the penman wishes to make use of. Such new-made letters have perfect harmony with the remaining letters of the original. The pen might even be used to suggest – with some assurance and reason – conjectural forms (for palaeographic or other purposes) where the originals were damaged or missing.

The pen will also supply appropriate and characteristic capitals to match any given small-letters (or lower case). Or, on the other hand, it will make proper small-letters to match any formal pen capitals. Similarly, the pen will supply appropriate numerals, signs, etc. to match any alphabet. In every case, this matching of formal pen capitals, small letters, numerals, etc. – for the present day scribe's purposes – can be perfect. Or the scribe may, if he choose, produce, by means of his pen, such complementary capitals, small letters, numerals, etc. to match their complementaries in some respects and to contrast with them in others (see Contrasting, below).

Contrasting

The formal pen – in the hand of one who understands the matching of letters – will supply capitals, or other characters, appropriately contrasting with the given text, or manuscript (and see Matching, above). Such contrasting forms are very useful for emphasis or other distinction.

Suggesting or inventing

All the uses mentioned above – some more, some less – involve suggestion prompted by the use of the pen. But, in all, the suggested invention or creation is produced in direct association with 'orthodox' skeleton or finished shapes. This is perhaps the widest and most useful range for pen-suggested creation. But a further familiarity with the qualities and effects of the broad-nib seems to hint at a legitimate changing and varying of 'orthodox' skeletons and finishes of our letters, very interesting to the penman, in which reshaping the broad nib itself might be chiefly instrumental.

In the past history of formal manuscript the broad-nib-in-use has effected such changes. One may reasonably suppose that legitimate developments will yet proceed from the broad-nib-in-experiment. And, moreover, the scribe, in order to keep his craft in vital health, must experiment in, and within, the proper use of his tools.

But, whether in dealing with the old or the modern, or, in anticipating the new, and whatever the degree of the penman's knowledge or skill, he will find that the broad nib, 'honestly' used, is an inexhaustible suggester of variety proper to itself.

Other uses

The broad-nibbed pen has other uses and many other possibilities. The planning or designing of monograms, cyphers and decorative (or decorated) letters and indeed any new or spontaneous variety of forms or arrangements of letters. Three other uses – that have great possibilities, and are of special interest to the penman – may be mentioned here:

Converting any other forms into pen forms

Ornamenting (or *Flourishing*, *Rubricating*, or *Illuminating*) of text, capitals, initials, or pages – in manuscripts, or in printed books.

Pen Drawing (plain or coloured) especially to go with, or to illustrate a manuscript text.

Part II   Formal Penmanship defined by its traditions

Chapter 1 The book-hands or manuscript letter forms

Definition by its traditions

Formal penmanship as practised by the modern scribe is founded on the ancient manuscript book and on the use of the broad-nibbed pen.

The books with which we are chiefly concerned are Latin manuscripts written on vellum. They date approximately from the fourth or fifth century to the end of the fifteenth century. Palæographers (i.e. students of ancient writing) call the formal hands in which these books were written, the book-hands, and the different kinds of book-hands are distinguished by various names, according to their shape and country or time.

There are many widely differing book-hands or manuscript letter-forms marking through the centuries the fashion of their time and country. We begin with books of the fourth or fifth century written in large roman capitals, either 'square' or compressed or rounded: these large letters are called majuscules. By the sixth century formal minuscules – or small letters (called by printers lower case) – make their appearance. At first the small letters are very round, but after 300 to 400 years they have become slightly compressed laterally and further developed in form; some of the tenth-century manuscripts closely resemble modern print. In Northern Europe these modern-looking letters gradually change, in the next 600 years, until they become the much compressed and angular black letter of the fifteenth century. In Italy, however, though the letters became stiffer they remained more open; and in the fifteenth century, by a revival of their earlier and better forms, Italian scribes produced a minuscule writing, with capitals to match, which became the model for the first Italian printers. Beginning soon after 1450, competition by the printers brought the practical production of manuscript books to an end about 1500. But formal penmanship continued in use, for various purposes, and fully developed italic writing appears in the sixteenth century.

The early printers, having no other models or ideas of books, necessarily copied – and copied closely – both the written characters and the 'make' of the penman's book; simply adapting them to suit their movable metal types and their printing-press: their object was to do the scribe's work, and to do it more quickly and cheaply. From the scribes, then, we inherit not only the general form and treatment of books, but the general characteristics of the three or four principal types which – not very greatly changed – we use in present-day printing.

In studying any of the many different Latin book-hands, we find that, notwithstanding their particular differences of shape and size and weight, they are alike in this – every one of them is a natural product of the broad-nibbed

51. Examples of four characteristic book-hands. Note: the first two examples represent remote – the second two, more near-ancestral-manuscript forms of our present-day printing types.

ROMAN CAPITALS
roman small-letters
italic small-letters
black-letter small-letters

pen, and each one of them can be automatically reproduced by us with such a pen, suitably shaped, held and moved. (See Part I, Chapter 5.)

Besides this common relationship through the broad nib, the different book-hands (of our special study) are all of one family – the Roman. Every one of them, however different in shape, is descended from the Roman capital of 2000 years ago, and, in each case, this descent can be traced by the student with pen or stylus in hand.

All our different types of letters being thus makeable creatures of the pen and traceable descendants of the Roman capital, we choose particular manuscripts and make a practical study of both their structure and their development. This experimental study is carried out with the help of an actual pen and the manuscripts themselves, or good facsimiles. It gives us, not only an intimate knowledge of the individual letters and the alphabets which we intend to make use of, but a general idea of natural form in letters and of some of the vital principles of letter making.

The special MSS for study

In acquiring his knowledge of letter forms, and in turning it to account, the scribe is guided by considerations of legibility and beauty, and by the current fashion or convention of his own time. He attempts in his work to carry out this generally accepted fashion as well as he can. It is open to him to find or suggest a better fashion (if he can); but the conventional shapes of the Roman capitals and of the Roman lower case are at present current in most parts of the world. The conventional *italic lower case* is also a widely recognized variety of the Roman alphabet.

These three forms – Roman capitals, Roman lower case, and italic lower case – are therefore of the first importance to the scribe: his main practice is concerned with their shapes – that is, with their characterized essential skeletons – which, by their common acceptance, constitute a temporal standard of legibility. In his study and practice, then, he aims at making these three particular letter forms as well as possible – and, perhaps, a little better – by small changes in detail directed at a more perfect legibility and beauty. In selecting his models from the ancient manuscripts, he chooses especially those manuscripts which have an obvious likeness or affinity with our present standard conventional letters.

ABCDEFGHIJKL
MNOPQRSTUVWXYZ

abcdefghijklmnopqrstuvwxyz

abcdefghijklmnopqrstuvwxyz

𝔞𝔟𝔠𝔡𝔢𝔣𝔤𝔥𝔦𝔧𝔨𝔩𝔪𝔫𝔬𝔭𝔮𝔯𝔰𝔱𝔲𝔳𝔴𝔵𝔶𝔷

52. Approximate, normal 'essential skeletons' of the most important modern forms of letters. Note: The skeletons give the plan of the letters, but we do not see the true shapes of the conventional forms until they have been characterized – by weighting and finishing.

The scribe also 'plays' with other forms of roman derivatives. There are, for example, a number of interesting varieties of what we may call 'black letter' hands. In Northern Europe, be it noted, conventional forms of black letters are still more common than roman types, and its very decorative form is still quite familiar to us by its frequent use as an 'occasional' type: it might indeed be reckoned as one of the letter forms in world-wide use.[1]

And the scribe may, if he is able, even venture out of the Roman family – on foraging expeditions, as it were – into Greek or other Eastern families. Such departures from his main theme may be made in order to find yet earlier relationships and more ancient families (Greek capitals, for example, are the ancestors of the Roman capitals); or, to investigate the contrasts and the similarities in different families (the letter-anatomist – like the biologist – in 'comparative anatomy' may find a clue to particular anatomy and function); or, it may be, to observe the native charm of foreign cultivation.

Such 'ploys' and expeditions among such different and distant letter forms may be attempted, and they may be attempted for direct profit or 'for the fun of the thing'. The adept enjoys experimenting with his tools, and the penman – equipped with his – can leave the beaten track and find such essays not unfruitful; nor is it indispensable for this that he should be familiar with any other language than his own and that of the pen.

Finally, whatever the ultimate purpose of our studies, the best way to study book-hands and other manuscript forms is to work at them as practical craftsmen specializing in the craft of formal penmanship. We may add with advantage some knowledge of the elements of illumination; but it is essential that, with our own hands and fingers, we produce manuscripts – whether decorative or decorated.

[1] E.J. writing in 1937. *Ed.*

Chapter 2 The physical structure of the ancient book or treatment of the pages

The best and most interesting practice is gained in the making of manuscript books. The fundamental technical aspects of their ancient form and treatment are of great importance to the modern scribe. As they form the groundwork of our craft, they are briefly tabulated on the opposite page.

We may well regard the book as the shrine devised to hold the written word; but we must bear in mind that its form and treatment have been evolved primarily for convenience in reading. It is also to the point to recognize that the acts of writing and reading are not only complementary but in many ways parallel, requiring proper conditions in many respects analogous.

Again, while the nature of writing has to some extent conditioned the form and treatment of the book, the physical limits of the book have imposed their conditions on writing. In fact the shrine and its precious contents have acted and reacted on each other (and continue to do so) until, in a sense, they have become indivisible.

Except in their substance and their substantial construction, the general physical form of the ancient vellum books is much the same as that of their descendants – our modern paper books. It will be sufficient then for our immediate purpose (the definition of formal penmanship by instances of its traditional models and methods) to describe here the inward physical and graphic structure of the ancient books.

Gathering the pages

Some notes on the structural treatment of Quires, Leaves, and Pages:
(a) The bulk of the Latin MS books appear to have been written on vellum – i.e. calf-skin (which, properly prepared, still gives us the best writing surface).
(b) Vellum has naturally a smooth (inner, or 'flesh') side and a rough (outer, or 'hair') side, or, more truly, a smooth and a less smooth side.
(c) Note: Both sides of the vellum were written upon.
(d) To make a book, sufficient sheets of vellum were cut to size, and folded.
(e) These folded book-sheets were gathered together into quires or sections.
(f) A section commonly consisted of four book-sheets, having, of course, eight leaves or sixteen pages.
(g) A number of these sections, stitched side by side to a series of bands, formed the bound book – minus its covers. (Note: The pages of the book – as produced by a professional scribe – would be prepared and written before binding, i.e. while the sheets in the section were still separate).
(h) The sheets in the section were so arranged that two 'smooth' sides came

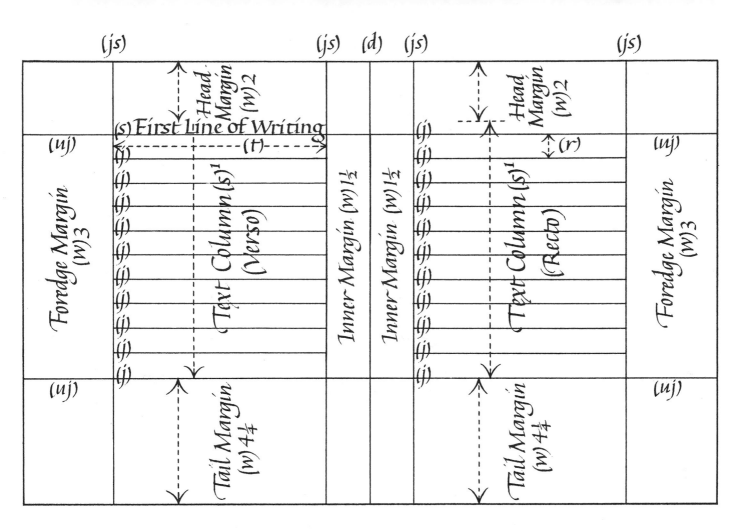

53. Diagram showing typical (main) ruling and marginal proportions of a prepared book-sheet (e). It may also be taken as representing the ground plan of an opening (i.e. any two facing pages) in a Medieval MS book.

The letters – in parentheses – correspond with the key-letters in the structural notes (pp. 131, 132, 133).

(d) Central fold
(s) Vertical marginal lines
(j) Writing lines
(r) Inter-line space
(s) Line of writing (i.e. the MS itself)
(s) Height of text column
(t) Writing line length (or width of text column)
(uj) First and last writing lines, projecting
(w) $1\frac{1}{2}$: 2 : 3 : $4\frac{1}{2}$: the four margins, as on the two facing pages, whose widths are in this ratio.
'Verso' = left page
'Recto' = right page

together and two 'rough' sides came together, alternately – so that in any given opening the two facing pages had similar surfaces. A second reason is that the skin tends to curve by its nature so that any tendency to warp in one way only is counteracted.

(i) Note: The scribe might prepare and pounce the writing surfaces, according to the nature of the vellum: this might be done before or after ruling, according to the nature of the ruling.

The ruling

(j) The pages were ruled with vertical marginal lines and with writing lines: all this ruling was permanent, and its lines became part of the visible structure of the page.

(k) In the earlier books the ruling was done with a blunt point, almost invariably on the rough side: this made fine grooves on the rough side of the sheet which appeared on the back of it (i.e. on the smooth side) as fine ridges.

(l) Thus also this ruling matched in opposite pages: grooved lines faced grooved lines, and ridged lines faced ridged lines, in successive openings. (See (h).)

(m) Note: The ruling was done before the sheets were folded – or at least with the fold flattened out: therefore, when the blunt point was used – making its impression right across and through the sheet – it ruled as many as four pages at one ruling.

(n) Note: Many of the early round hands were written between alternate pairs of lines, or between specially double-grooved lines – made, evidently, with a fixed pair of blunt points. Such ruling had an important reaction on the writing, affecting the shapes of some of the letters to a marked degree.

(o) Later (appearing first in the eleventh century) a metallic lead point is used, and, still later, the lines are ruled with a fine pen, in faint, or faintly tinted, ink.

(p) Definitely coloured lines were also used (in the fifteenth century) for their ornamental effect.

(q) The space between the writing lines was set, and kept very regular throughout the book.

(r) This inter-line space was different for different MSS, it was decided not only by the actual size of the writing to be used, but in accordance with the style of writing in use. About $\frac{1}{3}$ inch or $\frac{1}{4}$ inch was common in the fifteenth century, some line spacing was much larger, especially in the earlier books; some much smaller – in the thirteenth century, for example, to write very small and close, and to have eight, nine, or more lines of MS to the inch was common!

The marginal lines

(s) The vertical marginal lines, ruled on either side of the text column, and usually ruled from top edge to bottom edge of the sheet, were set to give a definite length to the line of writing fixed upon for a particular book.

(t) This writing line length – a very important 'constant' (or unvarying quantity) in the book – was decided jointly with, or in relation to, the size of the writing and the width of the vellum page. Their proper inter-proportioning provided a suitable length of line for the text, and a suitable side margin to the right and left of it.

(u) Above and below the text, the 'head' and the 'tail' margins were sufficiently indicated and determined by the positions of its first and last ruled writing lines. But, to enhance the marginal effect, commonly one (or more) of the head and tail writing lines were ruled right across the page, and made to show on either side of the text.

(v) The total area allotted to margins depended on various considerations: normal margins occupied from about three-fifths to five-eighths of the page area – the text occupying the remaining two-fifths or three-eighths of the page.

(w) The inter-proportions of the four different margins follow a system: they are given increasing width in order – inner margin, head margin, fore-edge margin, tail margin. A ratio, for these, of $1\frac{1}{2}:2:3:4\frac{1}{2}$, may be taken as typical.

(x) Note: The system of proportional margins based the width of each margin on its special nature and function. Though it gave the book a handsome appearance, its primary purpose was to be useful.

(y) Most of the old (Latin) books have one text column on each page, but some, especially later, have two columns to the page, with a more or less narrow margin between the columns.

(z) Besides the main ruling (referred to above), medieval MSS often show much duplication of marginal lines and the addition of extra and outer framing lines (such extra lines form a sort of link between what we may distinguish as basic structural treatment and the actual constructive graphic treatment which follows).

Chapter 3　The graphic structure of the ancient book or treatment of the text

The customary page-ruling, described above, is really the ground plan of the book. But it is more than a guide to the penman; it is the permanent foundation of every page, and it remains – after the book is written – a permanently visible and valuable feature of every page. Upon its lines all the contents of the book are arranged and the text is written, in the book-hand of the time, uniformly and evenly. But, after the book is finished, the ruled lines still show, however faintly, with useful effect, optically trimming the text, visibly supporting the 'architectural' quality of the pages and helping to preserve the unity of the book.

A good parallel to this two-fold nature of a manuscript – with its permanent lines and its text – is to be found in another craft. The web of the weaver is made of the warp and the weft, the threads of the warp are carefully planned and arranged in the loom; the weft is woven evenly throughout them: the make and the pattern of the woven fabric are dominated to a great extent by the plan and arrangement of the threads of the warp, though the weaver with his shuttle (like the scribe with his pen) has also great power and freedom of choice in the weaving.

The primary purpose of the scribe was to produce a readable book. In the use of his pen and in the treatment of his text he pursued this purpose – as a workman, aiming literally at usefulness – as far as was compatible with the natural conditions and traditional customs of his craft.

Note: In judging the readableness and the character of the ancient MSS we must remember this fundamental simplicity in the outlook of the scribe. And we must also remember that, during the first 1500 years of the present era, he was not only developing but inventing the form and features of the book as we know it.

The stage which book-development had reached in any given period must be realized. In very early books there were practically no text divisions: the text consisted of a series of columns of uniform lines of letters; even the idea of separating the words had not yet been invented – words were written as they were spoken, without inter-word pauses. By the seventeenth century the more important and familiar features of the text-treatment were present. By the twelfth century text-treatment had become more regularized, and the book seems to have attained a definite stage in tradition – standing midway between the earlier pioneer MSS and those of the later 'consolidation' and development. The minuscule writing retains some of the early largeness, but lateral compression has set in, and the MS is in consequence intrinsically less legible. Written capitals to match the minuscule letters – for writing 'proper names' etc. in the text – came into use about this time.

In the thirteenth century, shortening, as well as narrowing, produced very small heavy writing, marking the maximum of general compression. The loss in readableness (by reduced size and space) was further increased by the extensive use of innumerable contraction signs – a sort of formal 'shorthand' for prefixes or suffixes or intermediate syllables.

The scribes can hardly be blamed for this economic 'push'. It was partly a natural transition, partly a natural trend (finally defeated, to our lasting benefit, by the Italian scribes). And though the scribes were involved in it, to the extent of both making and following the fashion, their calligraphy was superb and their aim was still as simple and direct as a modern book printer's.

We cannot stress too much the fact that the scribe's direct aim was readableness. All the charm and delight of skilled and imaginative calligraphy in the ancient manuscripts and all the gorgeous wonders of their illumination – though, without doubt, an 'end' – are to be seen truly as the 'flowering' of a craft based on usefulness.

The line-of-writing

Some notes on the arrangement of letters in lines and columns, and the treatment of text divisions.

(A) Note: To the penman the line-of-writing is the characteristic unit of the book. The line-of-writing is, in fact, the essential element, and – more than any other part or feature – it characterizes the pages and gives unity to the book as a whole.

(B) The line-of-writing – in any given book – is constant in character throughout the book. Its three principal characteristics are:

Its (particular) letter-form and texture;

Its (proper) inter-line spacing;

Its (approximate) length.

Even texture

(C) The proper arrangement of letters in a line – or the proper writing of a line-of-writing – approximate to an even distribution of the strong strokes, giving the line of writing an even texture.

(D) This texture is kept uniform through all the lines of a MS. It varies in different MSS, and may be:

Open (as in many early MSS)

Medium (as in tenth and eleventh century and later Italian MSS)

Close (or compressed, as in the later English, French and German MSS).

(E) Inter-line spacing (i.e. the white open spaces between the lines of writing) commonly, and naturally, corresponds with the texture of the line of writing and is open, medium, or close, respectively, with open, medium, or close-textured MSS.

(F) Proper inter-line spacing is specially suited, in this way, to the letter form or texture or to the length of the lines, or to some special aspect of the MS. It commonly gives perfect clearance to the heads and tails, or ascenders and descenders of the letters in adjacent lines. But, more particularly it allows each line of writing a margin of white, or background, sufficient to give each line in the text column distinction. The lines of writing in the ancient MSS nearly always show as lines – even when seen from a considerable distance.

The text column

(G) The text column (i.e. the column of lines of writing on every ordinary page of the book) being built up of distinct lines of writing, appears like a striped fabric. The stripes may be very near together, in some MSS, or, in others, pretty far apart, but the striped effect is nearly always obvious. Note: It will be seen that, if we liken the text column to a 'patch', then every page, and so the whole book, will be characterized by these fabric-like patches, woven evenly and true to pattern.

(H) The lines-of-writing follow the ruled lines of the text column, which have already been set to suit the MS. In the weaving of the free writing on this rigid framework there must, of course, be some approximations. But, besides the constant characteristics of the line itself (B), two (or commonly three) other features of the text-column are fixed and so help to preserve the unity of the book:

The position on the page of the head line-of-writing:

The normal straightness (but see (J)) of the left side or edge of the text column and its respective 'verso' and 'recto' positions:

The number of lines-of-writing in the text-column (commonly constant; sometimes varied).

Note: The question of the 'constants' of the text-column involve a point of theory which is of some importance. Here, for clearness, the facts recorded above (H) may be expanded and restated thus:

In the case of any given MS book:

(I) All ordinary columns begin at the same page level. All ordinary lines of writing begin level (at a vertical line) on the left. But lines of evenly written MS cannot be made to end level on the right (without improper word breaking). The text column therefore has a more or less irregular right vertical edge (it may be compared to a banner flying eastwards, of which the eastern edge is somewhat tattered). All ordinary columns are commonly (but not necessarily) at the same page level.

The normal conditions may be summed up, simply, thus:

The text-columns of the MS book are like nearly similar, harmonious, striped, rectangular patches, each patch having three straight sides and one wavy side. And these patches are similarly placed – on their respective recto and verso pages – throughout the book. (Note: These MS columns may be roughly compared – in their general treatment and character and characterization of a given book – with the printed columns of a modern printed book. In all technical details, however, the written page and the printed page differ fundamentally, and their differences are most important and suggestive.

(J) Note: In some of the early round hands (of about fifth–seventh centuries), instead of all the lines of writing beginning level, there is a formal indenting (i.e. setting in) of certain lines, by one, two, or more letter places. This method was used apparently to mark verses or phrases, by lines, punctuation being then rudimentary or absent. To some extent the formal indentations on the left balance the accidental irregularities on the right (which the width of the round letters tended to exaggerate) and give an almost centralized effect to the lines of the column.

Text divisions

(K) Divisions of the text were generally marked by large brightly coloured, and decorated ornamental initials and by the use of capitals. Note: With the exception of some 'titling' in pen-capitals, this is practically the only use which the scribe made of capital letters in the minuscule MSS of about the sixth to the eleventh century. Such initials and the larger capitals were commonly measured by the lines ruled for the text; their height being many or few lines according to their degree.

(L) The book itself is commonly begun with a very large ornamental initial letter or word, which is followed by a line or more of large capitals, and sometimes these are followed by a line or more of simple pen capitals, immediately after which the text follows in minuscule. This ornamental beginning may occupy a large part of, or the whole of, the first page of the text.

(M) The beginnings of other text divisions, such as books and chapters and paragraphs and verses, are marked, in their degree, with large ornamental initial letters, etc.

The size and importance of these initial 'markings' approximately correspond with the size and importance of the text divisions. For example, while the initial ornament of the book frequently occupies the best part of a page, a *paragraph* is commonly marked by a single, decorated versal, several lines high, and perhaps a couple of small black pen-capitals (in the text), and separate *lines of text* may be marked by plain (coloured) one-line versals (or, later, by simple pen-capitals).

(N) Another device (which, though not actually textual, touches on the text treatment) is the ornamental line finishing. These ornaments were used to fill certain gaps at the ends of lines – such as the frequent verse-end gaps in a column of verses – not the occasional accidental gaps in ordinary continuous text. Figuratively speaking when, by the nature of the text, the normal tattered right edge (I) of the text column fabric ran into frequent rents, the line finishing mended or patched these rents and kept the fabric of the column whole. As an ornament at the ends of verses, it came to be treated as a sort of echo of the ornamental initials which began the verses. (Line finishing was notably developed in the twelfth century and after, and this development was probably the direct outcome of the 'compressed' MS of the time – which, by the contrast of its closer texture with the white background, showed up gaps in the fabric more vividly.)

Commentary on the above notes on traditional models and methods

The traditions of penmanship

The notes given above constitute an attempt, within the limits of three chapters, to define formal penmanship by its traditions – to show, in fact, what formal penmanship is, by a brief exposition of the scribe's traditional technique.

They deal mainly with some selected examples of the models and methods of the ancient penman, that is to say, with the forms of his letters and the making of his books.

The forms of the penman's letters: These pen-letters are found in the book-hands, which are many and diverse. The present chapter, therefore, gives only a short general account of their nature and use (under the subjects of book-hands, MSS for study, and text treatment). But their general construction – by thick and thin strokes – has already been described in Part I;
The making of the penman's books: The MS book has been dealt with, in the present chapter, as a sort of ideal book-form at which the scribes arrived, chiefly by considerations of practical use. The actual development of this typical book, the main features of its underlying methodical structure and of its obvious text treatment, are merely hinted at.

The craft of penmanship

Besides attempting to give a brief account of the ancient scribe's technique, I have tried to bring out the important truths – for the modern scribe. The first is that
Our formal penmanship is primarily a handicraft.
This fact is clearly implied in the present chapter in its record of a series of practical methods which constitute a systematic working tradition.

It has already been practically demonstrated in Part I, which shows how the tool – the broad-nibbed pen – dominates our writing. And it is upheld in Part III (and in the Forenote) where I have tried to further the intellectual conception of it by stressing the idea of direct useful purpose.

Handicraft – the true general term for such work as ours – covers both the ideal and the practical in it. Our ideals are craftsmen's ideals, our practices are craftsmen's practices. We work in substances; we aim at usefulnesses; we proceed by methods. This course does not prevent beauty being our ultimate aim, but it reaches beauty by these three steps – in the craftsman's way.

The place of penmanship

The second important truth for the modern scribe is, that
The manuscript book is the vital origin of the models and methods of our craft.
That this *was* so, is a matter of history. All our work, every element of it, was either born or bred in the book, and brought to a measure of perfection in it.

That it is still so, will be agreed by all serious students of our craft, for, with one accord, we make the MS book either the central interest, or the principal medium for our writing. We know that for us the book is still the best training ground and birthplace of ideas.

Besides his substances or tools, which tend in themselves to produce their special manipulative methods and natural forms, the craftsman requires, for his training and inspiration, a material purposeful object or thing which will impose its own natural conditions and suggest its own natural solution or treatment. By the practice of making such things he acquires trained skill and learns how to adapt his work.

For the penman this thing is certainly the MS book. In making it we learn our craft. In its general plan and principles it is ever the same. In its particular treatment it is ever new and changing with the problems presented by each new and different book. Mainly we follow the old methods and solutions, but often we are led or compelled to vary them and even to find new methods for ourselves. So we inherit the old traditions and so we invent new ones.

The book was and is the *sine qua non* of the formal penman. This necessity and its many virtues we must consider later. Here I say, briefly, only this: to us the particular value of the book is that it gives the most opportunity for freedom and variety under traditional control.

Part III   Formal Penmanship defined by the thing

Formal Penmanship defined by the thing

In the expression 'Definition by the Thing', the important word 'Thing' has a double sense: it means both *what we make* and *what we do*.

What we make refers to *material objects*, or, more exactly, to the idea of a *particular material object which has a particular use or purpose of its own* – as, for example, a particular manuscript-book, or a particular illuminated-address.

What we do refers to our *actions and intentions*, or, more exactly, to the idea of *what, all the time, we are doing or trying to do* – as, for example, writing well, or legibly, or freely (and to what end). These things are the subject of the following attempted definition of formal penmanship: they are *doings* rather than methods, though they pass immediately into methods. Their importance for us craftsmen is that our actions and intentions constitute the *soul* of the thing which we make; they are embodied in it and reflected in every aspect and function of it.

The word 'thing' as commonly used in this book refers to useful material objects.

Lest the student (perhaps excusably) mistakes the following statement for attempted *free verse* or for a simple list of platitudes, let me assure him that it represents a serious attempt to express a point of view, and to show in brief the outlook into which I myself have grown, and to which I believe any worth in my own work is attributable. The student must, of course, grow into *his own* outlook.

Forenote on the Craftsman

(a) The craftsman is one who works in substances, making things of them, with special tools and by special methods.

(b) He also thinks in substances and in things, and in methods – plans or designs – which direct the tool and form the thing out of the substance.

(c) He thinks of substances, things, and designs (methods, plans, etc.) as radically inseparable factors in his work.

(d) All his works express Idea (or feeling) by substance brought to life – like Adam made from Earth.

(e) Each one of his works – like every Son of Adam – bears a human touch, and is seen to be unique. All things are unique, but the craftsman's works show this – each one (each manuscript of ours) is an autograph.

The Nature and Purpose of Penmanship

Formal Penmanship is a handicraft:
The prime purpose of writing is to be read.

The Penman is a Craftsman:

His direct objective is to write well.

Writing well, for him, means making good use of his pen and his alphabets: it means writing clear, 'true' pen-characters fitted for the particular purpose, use, or function of the *thing he is making*.

The thing he is making is primarily useful:

Its uses and conditions suggest or prescribe its own proper treatment.

The *words* of the thing are of the first importance:

The scribe's ideal is to give the words perfect *presentation*.

Perfect presentation in writing approximates to perfect delivery in speaking:

Aiming at this ideal, the scribe's first duty is to his author.

The scribe usually aims at making this presentation *beautiful:*

But he also feels confident that good workmanship (either done or attempted) always has a measure of this divine reward.

The excellence – and beauty – of Formal Penmanship is achieved chiefly by three things

> SHARPNESS
>
> UNITY
>
> & FREEDOM

The nature of Formal Penmanship is essentially straightforward and swift,

So that normally the writing of the scribe simply flows on like the letters of a printed book.

Not only does the swiftness of *normal reading* require a general uniformity of flow, in the presentation of the text, approaching monotony,

But the swiftness of *normal penmanship* requires a corresponding uniformity of action, in writing a text, approaching the mechanical.

The good scribe cultivates such uniformity of action until it becomes habitual.

But simultaneously he cultivates an alertness (whether in pre-planning or later adapting) *ready to spring at a chance*.

Metaphorically, his penmanship – which is as swift and as free as he can make it –

Runs with the freedom of a channelled stream.

But there comes a fall or a bend in the stream,

And the stream leaps the fall, scours and widens the bend, and then runs on again.

Straightforward and happy penmanship exacts a minimum of thought –

Care-free (like the Spirit of the Stream) the happy scribe writes –

Care-free (like the Spirit of the Stream) he writes – pen in hand, racing with the text, his mind flying back and forth over the whole –

In an instant the pen leaps or twists, touching the straightforward flow with variety – from the common, less visible subtleties, to the rare, most striking significance.

Now, whatever varieties – whether anticipated in his original plan for the whole, or made on the spur of the moment, whether small or great, whether veiled or obvious – whatever emphases, fancies, or romances, the scribe *dares to introduce*, they are right, and right only, when they are directly to the advantage of the thing itself and to the words of the author.

Such changes or breaks in the flow of the text may involve either letters, lines, words, phrases, sentences, paragraphs, chapters, books, or other text divisions (or whole texts when specially planned throughout). They are in practice in the nature of *emphasis*, which the penman may distinguish as –

Emphasis of position or spacing or arrangement,

Emphasis of form or size,

Emphasis of weight or colour.

The direct object of emphasis is to give proper prominence to special parts of the text. It is a sort of *reasonable exaggeration*, stressing or accentuating the natural qualities and features of significant or suitable *letters*. Marking *important divisions* and *important parts of the text*, and, more rarely, attempting to give *distinction* (where in the original text it is not marked or only slightly indicated) *to the natural sense or force of the words*. (In this last venture, the daring scribe may sometimes 'take his life in his hand'.)

Proper emphasis is *in the first place useful*; it makes a text more readable, by clearly distinguishing its parts.

Take, for example, a common method: special *initial letters* were made originally – and properly, are still made – to *catch the eye* of the reader, and indicate *beginnings*: initial letters are, in fact, *essentially optical bookmarkers*.

But, when the work is properly executed, these emphases inevitably form decorative *contrasts* in the written page:

And the penman, who, by proper presentation, makes the *written words effective in respect of their meaning*, may often with advantage go further, and add to their *effective appearance*, by deliberately enhancing the decorative effect of these contrasts.

Briefly stated: decorative features which do not interfere with presentation, generally assist it. (Compare the *gestures* of an accomplished speaker.)

This stressing or heightening of the naturally decorative features of creation – these intrusions, liberties, and additions of the craftsman – may be regarded as doing more than is necessary, and, therefore, open to doubt.

But proper presentation involves more than simple legibility: it requires legibility proper to the writing,

Treatment proper to the substances, manipulation proper to the tools, making (*which includes legibility, treatment, and manipulation*) proper to the thing (*which bears or enshrines the essential words*).

And it is in these things – especially in the use of our tool, the pen, and in the making of purposeful things, bearing specific words – that we find our opportunities, suggestions, guidance, impelling compulsion and even necessity, which may rightly prompt or move us to make additions that are *real additions* to the work.

Now, in such enterprise, in adventuring beyond 'necessity', we face the delights and dangers of life:

The adventure is difficult, but the test is simple and severe –

Are our additions of advantage to the words and the thing, do they help or hinder proper presentation?

We find in these adventures that the treatment of the penman's useful and naturally decorative emphases, of whatever kind (for instance, such simple changes as 'flourishing' some of the letters, or writing some of them in colour) merge irresistibly and almost insensibly into the art or craft of illumination.

By the addition of such emphasis, we make the reading easier: by the enhancement of such emphasis we make the reading more beautiful.

143

We aim at, and above, legibility; we aim at readableness or making the written words easy-and-pleasant-to-read.

This, then, is the scribe's direct purpose – *The making of useful things legibly beautiful.*

The scribe keeps the idea of *usefulness* constantly before him.

Usefulness is the foundation and essential basis of all craftsmanship. And whether in its primal form, simple *legibility* (of the writing), or in its practical form, *fitness for purpose* (of the thing made), or in its ideal form, *perfect presentation* (of the words), we follow after usefulness and its ultimate objective, beauty.

Usefulness and beauty are the two ends of embodied truth:

Usefulness is the end that all can grasp;

Truth in the form of usefulness gives us a sovereign safeguard against the three sins which most easily beset us craftsmen: Against the danger of falling into faint-hearted *doubtfulness*, empty *mimicry*, or foolish *affectation*, we set the simple rule –

To be true to readableness, to penmanship, and to our author.

The scribe is equally responsible for any special plan which he has made for the treatment of a text as a whole, and for the details which he adds – whether indicated in his original plan, or coming as afterthoughts in its execution.

Even in a straightforward rendering of the utmost simplicity there is a personal touch, but, in any deliberate departure from such simplicity, the scribe is intruding his own ideas. This he may rightly do, if he keep to the terms of his safeguard: to be true to his letters, his pen, and his author will actually help him to be true to himself.

Whenever he makes a manuscript he is making a *single* copy. The unique and personal nature of such autographic rendering not only permits, but in a sense compels and makes desirable, a personal *feeling* in the presentation (comparable, in a modest degree, with the interpretation that the actor or musician may give to the works of their authors).

This separate and autographic making of every written page – stroke by stroke – and the manual freedom of our craft, which permits of our writing as readily in colour as in black, in large letters as in small, offers us almost unlimited opportunities for introducing variety and arrangement, form, and colour, and even extra ornament and illumination.

When they make for the good of the thing, for the help of the words, we take these opportunities as we will and can.

The scribe's rendering of a text is naturally individual and personal.

But his natural egoism is curbed by loyalty to his author's wording (as he understands it).

Therefore his great freedom of choice is made subservient to the production of a manuscript which, in whole or in part, is a sincere presentation of that wording, and is, as far as he is able, in sympathy with it.

And I believe that all that concerns special parts and letters – all that concerns special treatment of the thing, all that concerns variety, emphasis, or illumination – also concerns, but much more subtly, all the ordinary letters and parts of a manuscript: *so that even in his individual pen-strokes* the penman may be in sympathy with the words that he is writing.

And I believe that no rendering is too simple or too plain to embody and contain this sympathy. Uniformity cannot conceal it: uniformity, like service, is a condition precedent of freedom.

And though the expression of this sympathy may be scarcely visible in any of its parts, yet – as in all things built up of separate elements and parts – in the completed work their effects are joined together, and their intention is felt, animating the whole manuscript.

These things being so, by its service and freedom, Formal Penmanship gives almost unlimited possibilities of sensitiveness and beauty in the rendering of the written word.

And, if our work and our additions help the proper presentation of the words, if our making of the thing is good, if, in fact, we write well –

Then even the poets – the makers – may thank us.

Appendix: the original material for Formal Penmanship

This appendix lists the material made available to me by Priscilla Johnston, in order to edit and prepare for publication *Formal Penmanship*, from the papers left by Edward Johnston at his death in 1944.

His 'vellum-bound notebook' has been consulted and his 'Notebook' inscribed 'Edward Johnston, Cleves, Ditchling, Sx. (valuable notes from August, 1920).'

Early version of Formal Penmanship described by its Tools, Part I
1 typescript page, Forenote, dated 1939 and 1940.
20 typescript pages numbered 1 to 20 consecutively, includes dates from 1937 to 1942.
10 text figures.

Later versions of Formal Penmanship, Part I
(a) 3 typescript pages A. B. C. dated 1942 and 1944.
(b) 19 typescript pages numbered 1 to 19 consecutively, dated 1942 and 1944.
1 text figure. Figures 2 to 7 are numbered but diagrams are lacking.
(c) 3 manuscript pages numbered 1, 2, 3, and one page unnumbered, dated 1941 and 1942.
2 text figures similar to figure 1 in (b).
(d) 23 manuscript pages numbered 1 to 17, in addition 2 pages are numbered 14, 3 numbered 15, 2 numbered 16, and 3 numbered 17, includes dates from 1941 and 1942.
13 text figures.

The Three Primary Factors or Writing Conditions
9 manuscript pages numbered 1 to 19 consecutively, dated 1937 and 1938.
7 text figures.

Experiments with Twin-points
17 typescript pages numbered 6 to 22 consecutively, dated 1934 and 1938.
11 text figures.

Letter Form
8 typescript pages numbered 11 to 22, page 16 missing.
6 manuscript pages numbered 1, 3, 4, 5, 8, 9, undated.
4 text figures.

Using the Three Factors in Copying a Manuscript
6 manuscript pages numbered 10 to 15 consecutively, dated 1941 and 1944.
6 text figures.

The Seven Rules for Copying a Manuscript
7 typescript pages numbered consecutively 23 to 29, undated.
1 text figure.

The Value and Uses of the Formal Pen
4 typescript pages numbered consecutively 6 to 9, undated.

Formal Penmanship defined by its Traditions, Part II
24 typescript pages, and two pages of an earlier version, undated.
1 text figure.

Formal Penmanship defined by the Thing, Part III
10 typescript pages, undated.
Without text figures.

Editor's Note: Addendum to a paper on the labelling of exhibits

Edward Johnston came to London in the autumn of 1898 to research into scripts at the British Museum and to make 'living letters with the formal pen'. Enthusiasm for the Arts and Crafts Movement was high at this time; the foundations of it had been laid by Ruskin in the early nineteenth century, but it was the prodigious energy and inspiration of his disciple William Morris that brought it into being. The Movement aimed at social, moral, and cultural reform, and was opposed to the shoddiness and sheer ugliness of the mass-produced objects of industrialism. During the 1880's and 1890's it flourished on the inspiration of William Morris's vision of the new order brought in by socialism and a revival of the crafts.

The Movement found a visual focus in the Arts and Crafts Exhibition Society which was founded in 1888 and held its first exhibition in London that year. The aim of the Society was to give craftsmen in all branches of the applied arts the opportunity to show their work. The twenty-five members of the committee, under the chairmanship of Walter Crane, were mostly drawn from the recently established Art Workers' Guild. Among the founder members were William Morris, William de Morgan, and W. R. Lethaby, and there were distinguished exhibitors at the first exhibition.

William Morris, who died two years before Johnston came to London, had experimented in the 1870's with writing and illuminating books by hand, and a lecture by Emery Walker, given during this first Arts and Crafts Exhibition, inspired him to start the Kelmscott Press, but at this time no one was seriously working on formal penmanship, and calligraphy was an unknown craft.

Professor W. R. Lethaby appointed Johnston, himself still a student of the subject, to be in charge of the first lettering class at the Central School of Arts and Crafts, which opened in September 1899 with seven notable students. Together with their master this group became pioneers of the craft. During the next quarter of a century the practice and influence of formal penmanship grew and spread with the publication of *Writing & Illuminating, & Lettering* in 1906, and Johnston's teaching at the Central School, at Camberwell and at the Royal College of Art.

In 1932 during his Presidency of the Arts and Crafts Exhibition Society Johnston put forward a scheme dear to his heart, which was the careful and detailed labelling of exhibits, so that craft exhibitions might be more intelligible and interesting to the public. At a meeting of the Society in 1933 he read a paper entitled 'The Labelling of Exhibits', in which he proposed that labels should give, briefly, informative data concerning the construction or function of the exhibit, or the craftsman's aim in making it. He discussed sample labels for three works in a current exhibition: a lampstand and shade, an ivory carving, and a wood carving. When the Society published this talk Johnston was invited to write as an addendum a full description and a label for a piece of his own work. He chose to write on his Shakespeare Sonnet CXVI, which is illustrated in colour as the frontispiece to *Formal Penmanship*, and the addendum to his paper is reprinted here.

Johnston took infinite trouble over his own labels, he specified the materials used, explained the intention of the work and the limitations imposed on it, stated how far he thought he had been successful and what he considered its faults. His search for perfection and truth caused him to find fault with his own work and attention was often drawn to these shortcomings in the colophons which conclude his manuscripts.

Addendum to a paper on the labelling of exhibits

read by the President, Edward Johnston, at the Annual General Meeting of the Arts and Crafts Exhibition Society, 13 June 1933.

It had been my intention that one or two of the three photographs shown with this paper should, if they were printed, be reproduced with it. But some of our Council asked me to give instead an example of my own work and a suitable 'Explanatory Label' for it.

I recognise the justice of the request – 'Physician heal thyself' – and I have attempted to respond, although my craft – by its apparently less substantial and less useful nature – presents special difficulties in the way of descriptive labelling.

Preliminary statement

The three essential virtues or principles of Formal Penmanship are sharpness, unity, and freedom. When embodied in a manuscript these virtues make themselves felt – to our immediate consciousness – as explicit form and uniformity and ease of writing. An apprehension which goes below these surface appearances will recognise in them the principles underlying all the crafts.

To achieve sharp and explicit form the pen nib must be sharp-edged and sharp-cornered, and the ink and the writing surface must be suitable. The writing surface must be supple and be supported by an elastic writing pad so that the surface adapts itself to meet the edge of the nib and to receive the sharply-made – or clean cut – writing strokes.

The larger pens used in the example were steel nibs (about $\frac{3}{32}$ in. wide, and specially ground sharp by myself); the smaller pen was a turkey's quill sharply and finely cut.

The writing surface is vellum (calf skin) – the best and most receptive material for formal penmanship. And the hair side, which gives the most perfect surface, is used when writing is on one side only, as in broadsheets like the example shown. The surface is scraped with a sharp knife (by the scribe) until a fine velvety nap is produced and, either after or before ruling, is pounced with finely powdered resin (gum Sandarach) – both processes promote sharp-edged pen-strokes by repelling the ink from all but the *track* laid down by the broad nib of the pen.

The dark brown 'ink' of this MS is a mixture of Oxford Ochre (powder)+ Gum Water+some Ivory Black (cake)+a little Vermilion (cake). This makes a solid and opaquely-uniform and 'gritty' ink (a 'gritty' ink gives sharper strokes than a 'slimy' ink). The red 'ink' (in the three initial words and in the footnote) is Orange Vermilion (cake)+a little Gum Water.

The writing pad used was a quire of thick blotting paper.

In all my MSS my main intention is to give *proper presentation* to the words, in a form suited to the purpose of the thing or object which bears them. I think primarily of the *words-and-the-thing*. The appearance of the *thing* is an important but secondary consideration. I study the words and consider their meaning carefully, sometimes for a day or more, before writing them. And I take some pains to get an accurate or good version of the text to be transcribed.

My method is consciously eclectic. The MS is deliberately planned and adorned in an attempt to give a faithful and chosen graphic-presentation of the words. This is more interesting than simple transcription to the scribe, and perhaps, to the reader also. Though it may be taken as a scribal interference with a given text, I take the risk of its actually being so, or of its being thought so by some readers.

The thing or object illustrated here was made as a present for a particular person and occasion. It may be described as a *square panel containing Shakespeare's Sonnet CXVI written in dark brown and red, and meant to be hung on a wall.*

The text of this Sonnet is taken from the Doves Press Edition of *Shakespeare's Sonnets* (1909), which is reprinted 'from the first edition – 1609'.

In the primary intention of giving this Sonnet a proper presentation I marked the (separate senses of the) three quatrains by red initial words and *inset* the (separate comment of the) final couplet. The initial 'If' of the couplet is flourished for several reasons – chiefly it is intended to *separate the sense* of the couplet from, and at the same time to *attach its form* to, the rest of the Sonnet.

While most of my MSS are written in an 'italic' or in a free 'roman' hand, for this MS I chose 'black-letter', partly to convey the sense of an earlier day (although Shakespeare's works were all printed in roman type, I believe), partly to compress the Sonnet's shape laterally, partly for weight and force, and – indirectly – to *delay the reader* (so that each word should sink in), and partly for its rich appearance.

Incidentally I reintroduced the long ss of the original (though perhaps the second s of 'compasse' may have been round).

The narrow square frame (12 in. × 12 in.) was taken first. It was chosen partly for its own sake and partly to fit the Sonnet. The Sonnet then was made to fit the frame – the MS being frequently tested in the frame during the writing of it.

The secondary intention, in the whole treatment of the thing, was to produce *a richly decorated panel complete in itself* – rather than the effect of a piece of writing 'framed' (as it is called) as an afterthought.

To my thinking I have been fairly successful in carrying out my intentions in this thing. But there is one rather serious fault – which, however, is not so apparent in the original MS, in its brown ink, as in the photograph – the texture of the MS is *too uneven* (e.g., lines 8 and 9 have been too much compressed). An approximately even texture is always a virtue in writing, and, though some latitude may be taken in closely filled broadsheets, any necessary extra compression is best allowed to happen under compulsion *at the ends of the lines*. There is also another fault to confess, namely, the omission of a comma after 'barke'.

Some of the above data are compressed into a suggested 'label':

The 'THING': SHAKESPEARE'S SONNET 116 written on Vellum – A glazed
Panel for Wall Decoration.
NIBS: Steel, ground sharp & Turkey Quill, cut fine.
VELLUM: scraped & 'pounced' to keep Pen-strokes *Sharp*.
'INKS': Oxford Ochre & Gum & Ivory Black & Vermilion, & Rubrics in Orange
Vermilion & Gum.
CHARACTER: Black letter as reminder of Antiquity, and to compress MS laterally,
& for weight & force, & – indirectly – *to delay the reader*, & for its rich appearance.
The FRAME was chosen first & the MS made to fit it.
My INTENTION: 1st A proper Graphic Presentation of the WORDS, suited to the
'Thing': 2nd A Decorated Wall Panel.
COMMENT: I think Intentions fairly fulfilled. But a serious fault *Uneven Texture*
(V. lines 8, 9). E.J. 11.iii.'34.

[This is an explanatory label for the MS panel which appears as a frontispiece
in this book. *Ed.*]

Reprinted from *FOUR PAPERS* read by Members of The Arts and Crafts
Exhibition Society. Published for The Arts & Crafts Exhibition Society by
Longmans, Green, & Co. Ltd, 39 Paternoster Row, London EC4, 1935.

[In 1960 The Arts and Crafts Exhibition Society changed its name; it is now
called The Society of Designer-Craftsmen. *Ed.*]

Plates 5–23

Plate 5
One of four Winchester Formal Writing Sheets published by Douglas Pepler. The first four lines are written by Johnston in his Foundational Hand and the four lines below in a formal italic hand. Both scripts were developed by him from his study of tenth-century manuscripts, especially the Ramsey Psalter, BM, Harley MS 2904. The print is in red and includes a woodblock of lettering 'abc' by Eric Gill. Most of these sheets bear a date and this one was hand-written on 31 May/1 June 1918. Size 11 × 8½ in. In the possession of Heather Child.

Plate 6
Page from a demonstration notebook made for Dorothy Mahoney, *née* Bishop. On this page, dated 7 February 1927, Johnston has written with double-pencils his Foundational Hand, capital letters, numerals and ampersands. In the top left he indicates the approximate ratio of nib-width to letter height, and below, line spacing related to height of the lower-case o. A note in the centre near the top of the page draws attention to the importance of giving full value to the tail counter of capital letter R.

Plate 7
Page from a demonstration notebook made for Dorothy Mahoney, *née* Bishop. On this page, dated 20 June 1932, Johnston gives his Seven Rules for copying a manuscript:
1. Angle of pen to the line. 2. Number of nib-widths to height. 3. Chosen shape of letter (the circular, oval, flatsided or pointed O, on which a manuscript hand is based). 4. Number of strokes. 5. Order in which the strokes are written. 6. Direction in which the strokes are written. 7. The speed of writing.

Plate 8
Page 21 from Margaret Alexander's notebook when she was a student taking private lessons. Size of page 13 × 10½ in. Johnston lists the principle characteristics of Italic:
1. Compression. 1a. Angularity. 2. Branching. 3. Extension. 3a. Flourishing. 4. There is generally a slope forward. He demonstrates these features and writes an Italic alphabet with double-pencils.

Plate 9
Page 27 from Margaret Alexander's

notebook. The writing in double-pencils, suggestive of a Title Page, was filled in with green ink later but only in order to show the form of the letters. The notes in pencil relate to Simplifying the Problems of Illumination. Johnston writes: 'First and simplest is *one* letter (with varied special forms); one pen; one colour. If you have *two* different letters, and/or two pens, and/or two colours (let them be in each case markedly different). The combinations of one, and/or two letters, pens and colours, give eight mathematical formulae – and each is open to infinite variations (in its actual forms and arrangements): so seek simplicity and decide your formula before starting.'

Plate 10
Page 33 from Margaret Alexander's notebook. The twelfth lesson, dated 10 August 1932. Writing in blue ink, with diagrams and interpolations in green ink and pencil. On this important page Johnston is concerned with the Relative and Absolute measures of letters in Size, Weight, Colour (black to grey), and Form. A note on the right-hand side of the page reads: 'One of the ways in which this affects us scribes importantly is the relatively proportionally large O (though the letter is twice the height of the small o), the counter is four times as large as the counter of the small o, and shows a background of four times as much WHITE. Absolutely this makes a very important difference.'

Plate 11
Page 40 from Margaret Alexander's notebook, dated 13 July 1933. A free rendering made by Johnston of tenth-century formal writing, from the BM, Harley MS 2904, the particular script on which he based his Foundational Hand. The main text is in sepia with the smaller capital B in scarlet. The vivid heading is written in scarlet Rustic capitals. The small semi-formal writing in the margins is red and green. A note at the top bears on the form and rendering of the feet of small letters which Johnston says should be 'finished, plump and brisk' like the best of his below. He makes the feet of his letters here much more marked than in the BM, Harley MS 2904, see figure 28 in 'Decoration and its uses' (page 52 in this volume).
The note running up the left side reads:

'General criticism of this piece of mine, the lower case are a little crowded and crushed (a tendency with me); the lines of the MS (and the individual dots in threes) better far apart; it was written off with little more than a trial of the pen.' A note on the right side reads: 'Particular criticism of this page [H] stem went utterly wrong through colour being too thick. Large B is a little near the text; small B is a little far away.' The General Note at the bottom refers to the three preceding pages which deal with: Problems of Things to be Made and the approach to such Practice (self-set or commissioned); the proper Treatment of Panels and Broadsheets; the normal Treatment of MS Books, in contrast mainly to panels, but illustrating the principles of "the more Open the Texture the more Background". Background here equals all Marginal Spaces, namely, Inter-Letter, Inter-Word, Inter-Line Spaces and the margins of the page or sheet.'
The pages from this remarkable notebook reveal something of the qualities of Johnston as the teacher and craftsman: his mathematical mind; his ability to criticize his own work; his generosity, that made him spend six weeks after the last lesson going through the notebook to clarify every point and then add as a bonus the Benedicite page, with its free, creative rendering of the Harley MS.

Plates 12 and 13
Pages 3 and 4 of a calligraphic letter written to Paul Standard in April 1944, in which Johnston relates how his Foundational Hand was first worked out. By kind permission of Paul Standard the relevant portion of this historic eight-paged letter is reproduced; it reads: 'Today's contribution shall be these – which may, and perhaps do, speak for themselves. Weeded of their i.e. my faults (wh. require, at least the apology of my condition, and my position – in bed –) *these* represent my present notion of the most useful Pen Letters for general purposes, and especially for Study by Type Designers. I have marked some of *my* worst *wobbles* for example (in b, h and l) and some of *my* worst *asymmetric curves* e.g. (in g, and m & o). I have marked some – e.g. n and p for *sloping*, sloping is out of place in these Winchester letters, which tho' free are essentially formal and upright. Three of my

letters stand out as a little better than the rest viz. k, q and r. These letters are rather freely copied from & based on the Xth Century Winchester Psalter (Plate VIII in my book "W. & I. & L."). Note: the Tail of the y (like several other parts) had to be invented and I have found that I preferred it "left plain". My Palæographic studies have been very slight but I *venture to say* that I doubt if any other MS extant (save possibly another by the same Writer, unknown to me) that would make so good a Strain from which *to breed Varieties* of our excellent and readable Printers' "roman l. c.", as this Winchester MS which contains, as it seems to me the perfected *Seed* of our Common Print, and besides, marks of the NOBLE RACE from which it sprang. Indeed the links with the Roman Capitals are so fresh in it, that I had to straighten the back of the Winchester a and fill out its neck and loop and deglossate the e. (continued 1 May – sitting up, with B. on K.)'
[Board on Knee. *Ed.*]
'I must be more particular about this very important Alphabet, v. p.4 line 2. The *"copying and basing"* mentioned is of course mine. The letters given on pp. 3 and 4 are not to be regarded as final even original in the literal sense. They represent what I myself, in the course of about 40 years, have "made of" the letters in a page of the Winchester MS (as I call it) as chosen for me I think by Sydney Cockerell and *photographed by Emery Walker.*
(Reproduced in *The Imprint*, May 1913.)'

Plate 14
Sheets of sample alphabets were used by Johnston as a regular part of his teaching; the one reproduced here shows the Foundational Hand with capitals to match, and arabic numerals. Also the head-hook, foot-hook and lozenge terminals to pen strokes, and the Seven Rules for copying a manuscript. These aids to teaching were produced in numbers by a hectograph method, which accounts for the lack of sharpness in the writing. Some of these early class-sheets formed the basis of *Manuscript & Inscription Letters*, published as a portfolio of sixteen plates (five by Eric Gill) by John Hogg in 1909.

Plate 15
'To the Body', poem by Alice Meynell, written in black and vermilion on vellum, 1914. In the possession of Heather Child. Size 12 × 12 in.

Plate 16
A page of Roman capitals, based on the Square Capitals of the third–fourth centuries. Black on vellum. This was probably a trial for the Postscript to *A Book of Sample Scripts* made for Sir Sydney Cockerell and completed on 29 March 1914. Size 16½ × 10 in. In the possession of the Johnston family.

Plate 17
A gift to Francis J. C. Cooper, Esq., in return for the loan of a book. Written in vermilion on paper, 13 April 1928. Size 8 × 5 in.

Plate 18
Address to Professor W. R. Lethaby on his retirement from the staff of the Royal College of Art, written in black and red on vellum, 1919. In the possession of John Dreyfus, Esq. Size 12 × 8 in. This Address was not presented. Written on the back in vermilion is a:
'Colophon Explanatory 1918–19
It is by the Scribe's default that the Professor did not get this letter a year ago (Alas! He, who shewed the Scribe a better way than "Art", did not shew him a longer way than "Life".)
Nevertheless, that it comes a year late, may help to prove its authenticity – besides indicating clearly the source of the manuscript, it testifies to the fact that the Professor is still warmly remembered by the Staff. E.J. script. Sussex. July 1919 AD.'

Plate 19
Collect for sixth Sunday after Trinity. Written in black and vermilion on vellum in the Foundational Hand. An inscription on the back reads: 'Written out by E.J., 28 July 1919, because Mr Rinder asked him to be a good soul and write something for Mrs Rinder for 29 July.' Now the property of Mr and Mrs Frank Rinder's daughter. Size (inside frame) 5⅜ × 4⅛ in.

Plate 20
Opening twelve lines of Chaucer's *Canterbury Tales*; transcribed by Johnston in an English Book Hand of about 1380, in black and red on vellum, for presentation to Miss Louisa Puller by the Society of Scribes and Illuminators in 1926. Victoria and Albert Museum Library, L.1879–1964.

Plate 21
Perpetual Calendar. This was one of Johnston's last important manuscripts; it was devised and made for his wife's birthday in 1932. His label for it is given in own words:
'PERPETUAL CALENDAR (in Frame) written with a Bamboo on Paper; the Motto, the "Keynote", in free copy 14th C. Eng. MS l.c.; Days in Caps. (*Thorn* used for TH): "INKS" as my Sonnet MS. *The NUMBERS are written to match the MS.*, & because of *that* and because of their large pen-work being forced into small space, they have acquired a strong *MS character* (They are, in fact, the first decent Numerals made by me – in 35 years) NOVr is written *too Tall for Weight* – a common scribal fault. Four screens (one in use), for screening off unwanted numbers, are (too bluntly) written upon, *to pattern the surface of a different plane*. Made in 1932–'33. (Joiners are asked to regard the frame as a *Sketch* for a Frame.) E. J., 20. x. '35.' In the possession of the Johnston family. The paper on which the Calendar was written is mounted on card and varnished. The motto translated: 'Our Time is in Thy Hands'.

The sonnet MS referred to is Shakespeare's sonnet CXVI, Frontispiece. Size of Calendar 16½ × 11 in.

Plate 22
Draft for an inscription in the church porch at Kippen, Stirlingshire. Black manuscript written with a bamboo in indian ink; vermilion written with a steel pen, 1938. Size 18 × 8 in. Draft in the possession of the Johnston family.

Plate 23
The opening of a calligraphic letter written in a semi-formal hand to Bernard Leach, the master potter, in October 1943. Quoted from the letter:
'Enforced leisure has given me an opportunity of apologising to some of my Friends (& this is what I call a *Handsome Apology*– espy. the Initials B and L . . . wh. have features that charm me almost & that I have never before seen or written) This makes the 7th Apology sent & a few more are due (I hope to pay abt. ¼d in the £1 in Apologies) – (besides it is rather fun doing them).
p.p.p.s. 27th Oct. '43
The more I look at the opening – espy the Initials B.L. – of this, the better I like it or them. I think they are the best I have ever done so far, & shd. w. yr. permission, like to have a photograph (For my book) of the Opening & down to the end of 2nd line of small M.S. ending with "apologise", i.e. *everything of the Beginning above the horizontal fold of the paper* (full size).'
Bernard Leach records 'I gave the original E.J. letter, at his earnest request, to Dr Soetsu Yanagi for his National Craft Museum of Japan'.

Plate 5

Et haec scribimus vobis ut gaudeatis, & gaudium vestrum sit plenum.

Et haec est annunciatio, quam audivimus ab eo, & annunciamus vobis : Quoniam Deus lux est, & tenebrae in eo non sunt ullae.

Henry "Italics" based on Winchester MS. Winchester MS. very slightly modified.

Note: This copy is written with a pen, not printed Ef. 31 May–1 June 1918. A.D.

In order that a child may learn how to write well the teaching of handwriting should begin with the practice of a Formal Hand. This Manuscript is written with a BROAD-NIBBED PEN which makes the strokes thick or thin according to the direction in which it moves. The strokes are generally begun downwards or forwards & the letters are formed of several strokes *(the pen being lifted after each stroke)*: thus *c* consists of *two* strokes, the first a long curve down, the second a short curve forward. The triangular 'heads' (as for *b* or *d*) are made by *three* strokes; 1st. a short thick

curve down, 2nd. a short thin stroke up *(the nib for this stroke being placed on the beginning of the first and slid up to the right)*, 3rd. the thick straight *stem* stroke of the letter itself down *(the pen for this stroke not being lifted)*.

Broad-nibbed steel pens and Reeds may be used: Quill pens are very good but require special cutting. How to cut Quill and Reed pens may be learned from my Handbook "Writing & Illuminating, & Lettering" *(John Hogg, London: 6s. 6d. net)* besides how to make MS. Books and to write in colour. Edward Johnston: *Ditchling, Sussex.*

THIS SHEET IS PUBLISHED BY DOUGLAS PEPLER at HAMPSHIRE HOUSE HAMMERSMITH 1916 A.D.

Price 5/-

Reduced on a/c of erasures to 2/6

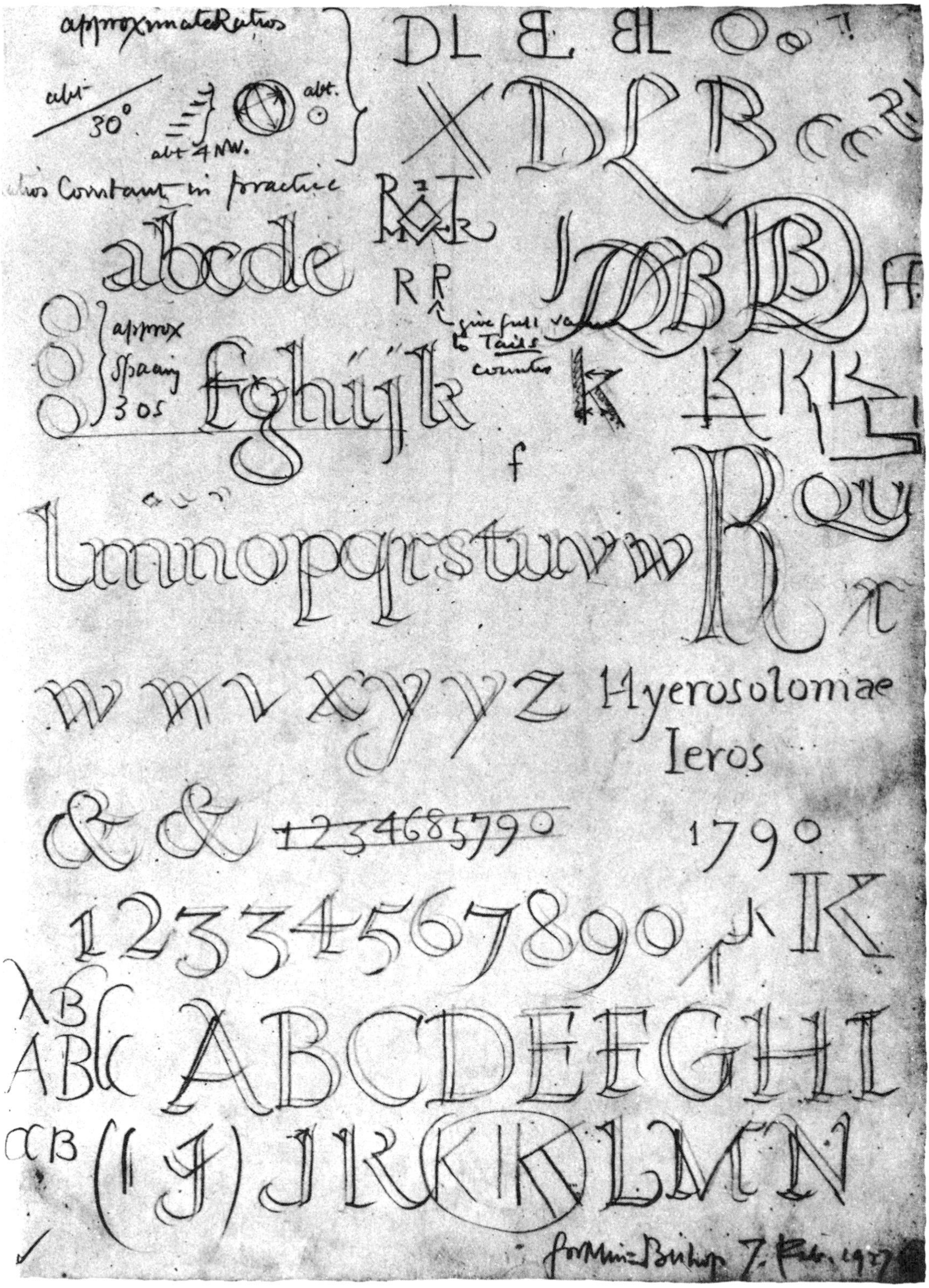
approximate Ratios
abt 30°
abt 4 NW.
Ratios Constant in practice
approx Spacing 30s
give full value to Tails counters
Hyerosolomae
Ieros
1790
1234567890
ABCDEFGHI
IJKLMN

Plate 6

Rules for Copying a MS. P.7. 20. June 1932

1.st
Angle
(to ----)

2.nd
Height
(to weight)

3.rd
Shape
selected (chosen)

(4.) Number (3)

5. Order (1st 2nd 3rd)

6 Direction

7th The (same) Speed

Circular   Oval   Flatsided   pointed

Plate 7

ITALICS

? 21

Plate 8

(? 2.) un continued — I think)

Note: There was
Lesson (the 3rd
1934 or total 7th)
the 10th June
...ly concerned
...scraping
...ing
...um surfaces
...also touching
...s (Eg supplement
...10th June lesson
...rough large
...MSS. on paper)
...in this little Book
...to bear the date
...June (tho'
...was
...dated
...
...tinuation
...June ?)

① Compression (@ "angularity")
② Branching
③ Extension
③a. Flourishing
④ There is generally a slope forward

28 May 1932
③ Tendency to Vertical Extension — decreases "Angle"

& Compressed

Foundational hand
Ideal, "circular O"

This is O somewhat as people "think of it"

① examples of compression
②

examples of branching

seraphim

Normal seraphim

k kk

abcdefghijklmn

nopqrstuvwxy

yz

compression

doubtful type
W W

2. { I think is responsible for 3 also, perhaps, being less subtle required emphasis in ascenders & descenders

so we arrive at ③

& ③a follows naturally... ending long strokes

ph ph
Normal Extension

marked Extension (but too stiff) also

ph

phil

Extended & flourished

Normal (n) V R

Flourished Extension

Compare with...

2nd stroke of V parallelled with ...

(n) V compressed

V compressed & parallel with ...

extra g
but R

"Italic"

Will you try less compression & angularity or more? Make up your mind how...

1st extension

extreme limit of compression

(c c e n n)

(I don't remember what illustrated by these, unless it was slight variation types of & angular finish.)

SIMPLIFYING PROBLEMS

(compare the general of 7.18.)

(note that ms. below is all l.c. only)

8 { One letter (with varied special forms) [or with its own Caps]
One pen
One colour

comments on a Title p.

Simplest

L'Allegro

If you have { Two letters (different)
xor Two pens
xor Two colours } Let them be in each case markedly different

with two l-p-cc.

Combinations of one or two letters give 8 formulas thus — pens & colours

0	1	2	2	1	2
2	1	1	2	1	1	2
2	2	2	1	2	1	1

E.G. "Big" & "Small"
or "Bright" & "Dark"

&

(thus the formula is open to infinite variation in its actual forms & arrangements): to seek simplicity decide your formula before starting!

il Penseroso

john milton → (centre)

?

a a á Milton or m

[The outline letters filled in to make them show up 18-Sep-31.]

Plate 9

Wednesday (sic) 10th August 1932.

Relative & Absolute measures (Size¹ Weight² (Form⁴ colour³))

4 NW.   8 NW

penstrokes Absolutely same weight (in I. & II.)
But the Letters' weights are Relatively different (II. is relatively, a lighter letter than I.)

ⁱⁱ is twice as long as ⁱ
ⁱⁱⁱ " " " " ⁱⁱ

Here considered as a letter O, for example, Ⓛ is 2ce the Height of Ⓢ, & Ⓛ's penstrokes are twice the width of (SS) penstrokes (= weight)
∴ These two O's are therefore Relatively in the same proportion of Height and weight

Now considered Absolutely
(L's strokes are heavier than S's, of course)
Ⓛ is FOUR times as large as Ⓢ

Measured in the Narrower nib (SS) penstroke unit, or lozenge, ◆ (·)

Area of Ⓛ 64 units & Area of Ⓢ = 16 units

One of the Ways in which this affects us scribes importantly —
In the (Relatively proportioned) "Large O," (though the letter is 2ce the height (&c.) of the "Small O") the "counter" is Four times as large as the "counter" of the small O.

& shows a background of FOUR times as much "WHITE"

Absolutely, this makes a v. important difference

Criticism of G. Foster Stent'. Book/
Heavy Caps look rather too heavy
Writing Too Spread out (look at & compressed sideways)
too t in of each letter (for Space) in the longline = abt 3/8 in. off the whole

T v. S.
(remember, easier to use simple contrast of Size without weight)

Title pages over

The 7. lines of MS. below are a sort of bonus, chiefly intended to bear critically on some of MS.'s formal MS.: Of the same sort I cannot remember what my criticism was, exactly, but it had particularly to do with an unsatisfactory form or rendering of the feet of the small letters (wh. were scamped, or crushed or draggled in appearance—these epithets!) and not finished, plump & brisk — like the best of mine below). My letters' feet here though right in spirit show more ill made ones than good ones: but good examples can be picked out (in 1st line all except last 2 Rs): 2nd line, 3rd foot of m/3rd, 1st of 5th m.//

4th f of 1st aa
5th f. 4 i
6th none i. last f. 8.
7th f. f. last i & n (1st) passable

HYMNUS TRIUM PUERORUM

Benedicite omnia opera

domini domino :.

laudate & super exaltate

eum in secula :. :.

Benedicite angeli domini

dn̄o. b celi domino .

General Criticism of this p. Amin. The l.c. are a little crooked (crowded): (a tendency with me) The lines of MS. (& the individual dots in :) fall a bit apart; & was written straight off with little more than a trial of the pen. Cant compare pp. 43 min.

Particular crit. of this p. b stem word utterly wrong through colour being too dark. Long B is a little mean—the text small. B in a little too narrow. 13.vii.33

GENERAL NOTE ON THE FOUR PP. 37, 38, 39, & 40.// first, third, second. In pp. 37.38.39. (to be Read in the order 37. 39. 38.) All the black ink & lead pencil Notes (& probably some Red Chalk) are the original Notes &c. of 30. May 1933.// The Red & Green ink (& probably the blue chalk) are added Explanatory Notes & Comments made by E.J. from 2.vi. to 15.vii.33.// P.37. deals with Problems of Things to be Made & the approach to such Practice (self-set or commissioned).// P.39. deal with proper Treatment of Panels or Broadsheets—(brought out in 3. criticisms of MA's 3 panels).// P.38. gives Normal Treatment of MS. Books (in contrast: mainly panels—but illustrating the principle of the more Open the Texture, the more the Background...

Plate 11

Plate 12

rstuvwx

These Letters are rather freely copied from & based on

xyz

the Xth Century Winchester Psalter (plate VIII in my Book "W. & I. & L."). Note: the Tail of the y (like several ~~others who appeared~~ had to be invented and I found that I preferred it "left plain"

My Palaeographic studies have been very slight but I venture to say that I doubt if there is any other MS. extant (save possibly another by the same Writer, unknown to me) that would make so good a Strain from which to breed Varieties of our excellent and readable Printers' "roman l. c.", as this Winchester MS. which con-tains, as it seems to me the perfected Seed of our Common Print,

Plate 13

The Modified 10th Century Winchester MS. or the (Roughly Written by E.J. 9 July 9)
"Foundational Hand"

X ≈ o abcdefghijkl

mnopqqrrrstuvw

xyyyyz& 12333455

677890 ("Arabic" Numerals made to match)
Varieties may be introduced in many
of these forms: besides the 2 qs &
different 3s 5s & 7s & modified 1s above

e.g. dffgmnpkxz &c.

Capitals may be made to match (from any type of skeleton as from ABE or
ABE or E, or ABE or E or from any recognizable shape) : made
with the same pen & in proportion they are bound to go with the small letters
whether in harmony or in contrast

bB Agree Also AA

CCDDEEEFFGG

HhIIJJKRLLS

O I I : : o Head or Foot hooks] = pen lozenges slightly curved
Heads

Seven Rules for Copying { Keep the same (1) Angle (2) Height (3) Shape
Manuscript { (4) Number (5) Order (6) Direction of strokes
& write at the same speed (or as near as you may)

Plate 14

THOU inmost, ultimate
Council of judgement, palace of decrees,
Where the high senses hold their spiritual state,
Sued by earth's embassies,
And sign, approve, accept, conceive, create;
Create— thy senses close
With the world's pleas. The random odours reach
Their sweetness in the place of thy repose,
Upon thy tongue the peach,
And in thy nostrils breathes the breathing rose.

To thee, secluded one,
The dark vibrations of the sightless skies,
The lovely inexplicit colours run;
The light gropes for those eyes.
O thou august! thou dost command the sun.

Music, all dumb, hath trod
Into thine ear her one effectual way;
And fire and cold approach to gain thy nod,
Where thou call'st up the day,
Where thou awaitest the appeal of God.

Alice Meynell

Plate 15

ETOSTENDITMIHIFLVIVM
AQVAEVITAESPLENDIDVM
TAMQVAMCRYSTALLVM
PROCEDENTEMDESEDEDEI
ETAGNI.INMEDIOPLATEAE
EIVSETEXVTRAQVEPARTE
FLVMINISLIGNVMVITAEAF
FERENSFRVCTVSDVODECIM
PERMENSESSINGVLOSRED-
DENSFRVCTVMSVVMETFO-
LIALIGNIADSANITATEM
GENTIVM.

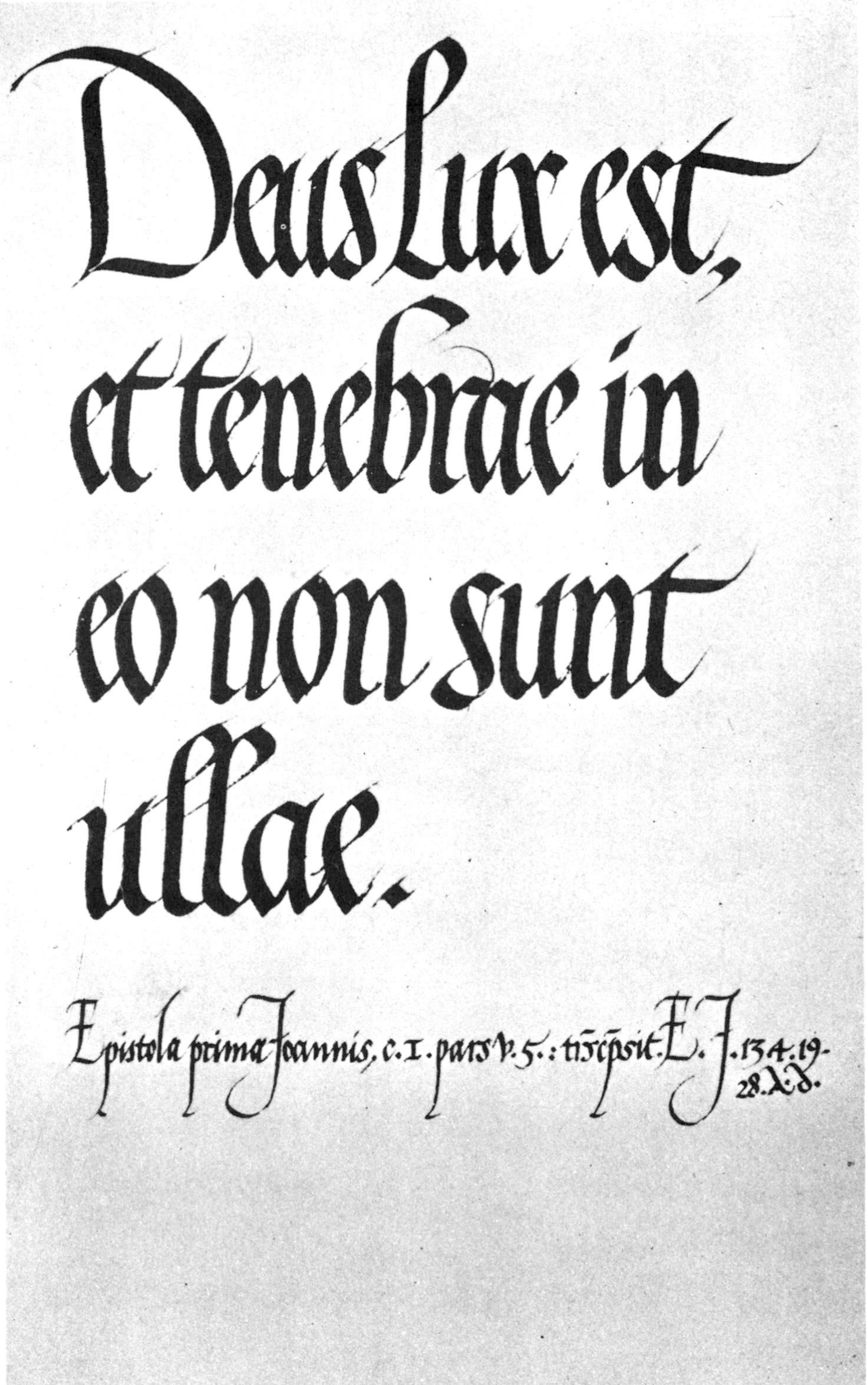

Deus Lux est,
et tenebrae in
eo non sunt
ullae.

Epistola prima Joannis, c.I. pars v.5.: tīscpsit E.J. 13.4.19.
28.X.8.

Plate 17

Royal College of Art

South Kensington, London.   August, 1918

To Professor W. R. Lethaby from the Staff
of the Royal College of Art.

Dear Proffessor Lethaby,

Your retirement is a matter of great concern to us. We are truly sorry that you have to leave us and your loss makes us look forward with some anxiety to the future when we shall try to continue rightly the work so largely begun by You. But now we wish to thank you, and to bless you in return, for what you have done for us.

While innumerable difficulties and doubts must beset achievement — obstacles when a man is striving and uncertainties when he looks back & contemplates his work — we should like you to know and to be certain of this: that you have earned the respect and affection of every one of us and that you have strengthened our faith and courage.

Plate 18

In matters both of Faith and of Works
you have always inspired us, and to know that you
were with us helped to give us confidence in our own
tasks and in each other. You cannot know how
much you helped us — particularly by encour...
all our efforts to do good and real work (howev...
feeble the worker's skill or its results). And, besid...
this, all of us who have asked you for help have
reason to remember some personal kindness on your part.

We hope that when you have left us
you may not see the lessons you have taught us mis-
applied or perverted, but that you may see their
fruition in works that at least come near achievement and aspire to goodness and reality.

July, 1919. We are, YouRs sincereLy,

O GOD, who hast prepared for them that love thee such good things as pass man's understanding; Pour into our hearts such love toward thee, that we, loving thee above all things, may obtain thy promises which exceed all that we can desire; through Jesus Christ our Lord.   Amen.

Collect for 6th Sunday after Trinity (27th July. 1919.)
X.D.

Plate 19   Plate 20

Here biginney ye Book of ye Tales of Caunterbury.

Whan yat Aprille Wiy his shoures sote ,

Ye droghte of Marche hay perced to ye rote ,

And hayed euery veyne in swich licour ,

Of Which vertu engendred is ye flour ,

Whan Zephirusbeek Wiy his swete hreey ,

Inspired hay in euery holt and heey ,

Ye tendre croppes and ye yonge sonne ,

Hay in ye Ram his halfe cours yronne ,

And smale fowsles maken melodye ,

Yat slepen al ye night Wiy open ye ,

So prikey hem nature in hir corages .

Yan Longen folk to goon on pilgrimages .

Geoffrey Chaucer (c. 1340-1400. A.D) wrote these words about 1386. A.D probably at Greenwich (as conjectured by Skeat pp. xvij & xiij). They are here transcribed in a fine copy of an English Bast Hand of about 1386. X. D.

The Prologue as given by Skeat

Here biginneth the Book of the Tales of Caunterbury.

WHAN that Aprille with his shoures sote
The droghte of Marche hath perced to the rote ,
And bathed every veyne in swich licour ,
Of which vertu engendred is the flour ;
Whan Zephirus eek with his swete breeth
Inspired hath in every holt and heeth
The tendre croppes and the yonge sonne
Hath in the Ram his halfe cours y-ronne ,
And smale fowles maken melodye ,
That slepen al the night with open yë ,
(So priketh hem nature in hir corages): ,,
Than longen folk to goon on pilgrimages ''
f: .... and specially .. to Caunterbury ..}

Though in its size the writing is about four times as tall as the 1386 Book Hand (in Chaucer's time the twelve lines might have been written in a space of about five square inches), yet the shapes of the Letters may be taken as somewhat like the characters in which the Tales must first have been written in a Book. The text is taken from Skeat's Student's Chaucer (1897) v. opp~ but his punctuation is omitted and replaced by line-end marks and certain letters are changed in form to the contemporary usage : thus Y = th, ſ = s (initial or medial) , but final S = 6 , and u = u. or v. (medial or final) , but initial u. or v. = V

Twelve Lines hit late Scriveyn for to redde ,
Edward a scribe , by ordre of ye redde ,
In nineteen hundred twenty seven Aprille ,
Wrote out Wiy yren and Wiy fowses Quille.

For presentation to Miss Louisa Puller this is written for the Society [or Guild] of Scribes & Illuminators by me.

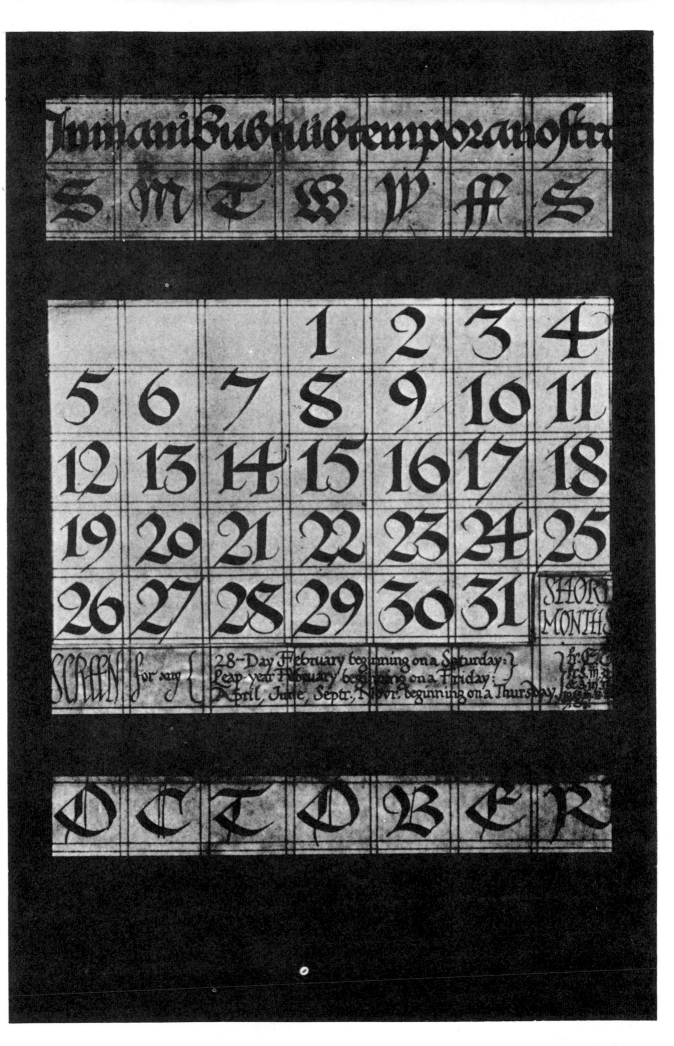

Plate 21

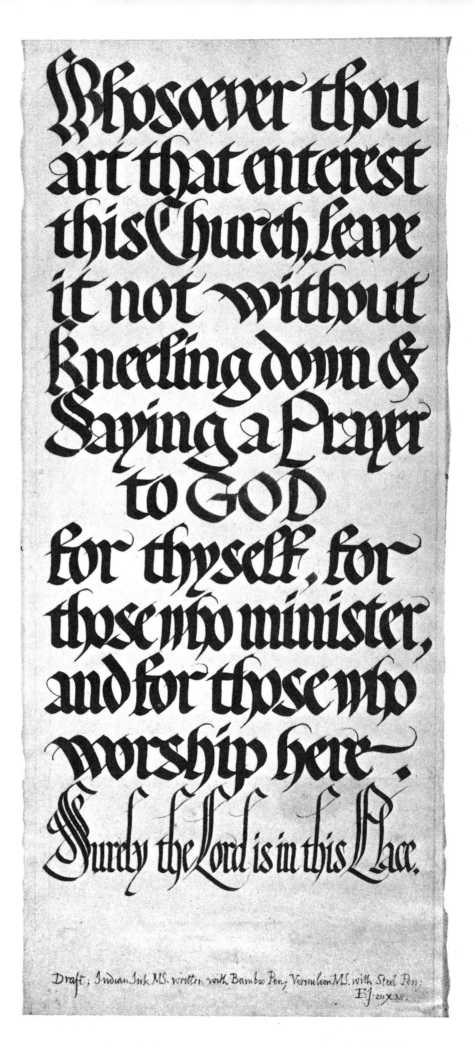

Whosœver thou art that enterest this Church, leave it not without kneeling down & Saying a Prayer to GOD for thyself, for those who minister, and for those who worship here. Surely the Lord is in this Place.

Draft; Indian Ink MS. written with Bamboo Pen; Vermilion MS. with Steel Pen; E.J. 20 x 28.

Plate 22

Ditchling
20. Octr.
mcmxliij.

BL

Dear Bernard Leach

this is to thank you for your
kind Note of the 11th. & to apologize
for keeping your LAO TZU so long;
& also to let you know something of my
State of Health —: Namely, that my
feet are very uncertain (walk tripedally)

unless a diagnosis

Plate 23

Index of names